MARRIAGE

SEASONS OF GROWTH

		ENTRY LEVEL	ADVANCED LEVEL
SESSION 1	**Getting Acquainted**	The Wedding at Cana John 2:1–11	
SESSION 2	**For Better or Worse**	Humble Beginnings Luke 2:1–7	Hard Times James 1:2–12
SESSION 3	**Love, Honor, Cherish**	Adam and Eve Genesis 2:18–25	Tough Act to Follow Philippians 2:1–11
SESSION 4	**Please Pass the Roles**	The Jesus Model John 13:1–17	Submit One to Another Ephesians 5:21–33
SESSION 5	**Baby Makes Three**	The Trip That Was Luke 2:41–52	Children, Obey Your Parents Ephesians 6:1–9
SESSION 6	**One Flesh**	An Ode to Love Song of Songs 1:16; 2:1–7; 4:1–7	Belonging to Each Other 1 Cor. 6:12–7:5
SESSION 7	**Till Death Do Us Part**	A Trick Question Matthew 19:1–12	Maturing Love 1 Corinthians 13:1–7

Serendipity House / P.O. Box 1012 / Littleton, CO 80160

TOLL FREE 1-800-525-9563 / www.serendipityhouse.com

99 00 01 02 / **101 series • CHG** / 5 4 3 2

PROJECT ENGINEER:
Lyman Coleman

WRITING TEAM:
Richard Peace, Lyman Coleman, Matthew Lockhart, Andrew Sloan, Cathy Tardif

PRODUCTION TEAM:
Christopher Werner, Sharon Penington, Erika Tiepel

COVER PHOTO:
© 1998 Bill Ross / Westlight

CORE VALUES

Community:	The purpose of this curriculum is to build community within the body of believers around Jesus Christ.
Group Process:	To build community, the curriculum must be designed to take a group through a step-by-step process of sharing your story with one another.
Interactive Bible Study:	To share your "story," the approach to Scripture in the curriculum needs to be open-ended and right brain—to "level the playing field" and encourage everyone to share.
Developmental Stages:	To provide a healthy program in the life cycle of a group, the curriculum needs to offer courses on three levels of commitment: (1) Beginner Stage—low-level entry, high structure, to level the playing field; (2) Growth Stage—deeper Bible study, flexible structure, to encourage group accountability; (3) Discipleship Stage—in-depth Bible study, open structure, to move the group into high gear.
Target Audiences:	To build community throughout the culture of the church, the curriculum needs to be flexible, adaptable and transferable into the structure of the average church.

ACKNOWLEDGMENTS

To Zondervan Bible Publishers
for permission to use
the NIV text,
The Holy Bible, New International Bible Society.
© 1973, 1978, 1984 by International Bible Society.
Used by permission of Zondervan Bible Publishers.

Questions and Answers

PURPOSE

1. **What is the purpose of this group?**

   In a nutshell, the purpose is to get acquainted and to double the size of the group.

STAGE

2. **What stage in the life cycle of a small group is this course designed for?**

   This 101 course is designed for the first stage in the three-stage life cycle of a small group. (See diagram below.) For a full explanation of the three-stage life cycle, see the center section.

GOALS

3. **What is the purpose of stage one in the life cycle?**

   The focus in this first stage is primarily on Group Building.

GROUP BUILDING

4. **How does this course develop Group Building?**

   Take a look at the illustration of the baseball diamond on page M5 in the center section. In the process of using this course, you will go around the four bases.

BIBLE STUDY

5. **What is the approach to Bible Study in this course?**

   As shown on page M4 of the center section, there are two options in this book. Option 1 is the light track, based on stories in the Bible. Option 2 is the heavier track, based on teaching passages in the Bible.

THREE-STAGE LIFE CYCLE OF A GROUP

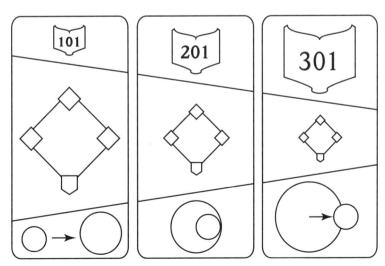

CHOOSING
AN OPTION

6. **Which option of Bible Study is best for our group?**

Option 1 is the best choice for people not familiar with the Bible, as well as for groups who are not familiar with each other. Option 2 is the best choice for groups who are familiar with the Bible *and* with one another. (However, whenever you have new people come to a meeting, we recommend you switch to Option 1 for that Bible Study.)

CHOOSING
BOTH OPTIONS

7. **Can we choose both options?**

Yes, depending upon your time schedule. Here's how to decide:

STUDY	APPROXIMATE COMPLETION TIME
Option 1 only	60–90 minutes
Option 2 only	60–90 minutes
Options 1 and 2	90–120 minutes

13-WEEK
PLAN

8. **What if we want to do both Options 1 and 2 but don't have time at the session?**

You can spend two weeks on a unit—Option 1 (the Story Questionnaire) the first week and Option 2 (the Epistle Study) the next. Session 1 has only one Bible Study—so you would end up with 13 weeks if you followed this plan.

BIBLE
KNOWLEDGE

9. **What if you don't know anything about the Bible?**

No problem. Option 1 is based on a parable or story that stands on its own—to discuss as though you are hearing it for the first time. Option 2 comes complete with reference notes—to help you understand the context of the Bible passage and any difficult words that need to be defined.

THE FEARLESS FOURSOME

If you have more than seven people at a meeting, Serendipity recommends you divide into groups of 4 for the Bible Study. Count off around the group: "one, two, one, two, etc."—and have the "ones" move quickly to another room for the Bible Study. Ask one person to be the leader and follow the directions for the Bible Study time. After 30 minutes, the Group Leader will call "Time" and ask all groups to come together for the Caring Time.

10. **What is the mission of a 101 group?**

Turn to page M5 of the center section. This course is designed for groups in the Birth stage—which means that your mission is to increase the size of the group by filling the "empty chair."

11. **How do we fill the empty chair?**

Pull up an empty chair during the group's prayer time and ask God to bring a new person to the group to fill it.

12. **What are the ground rules for the group?** It's very important that your group discuss these rules—preferably as part of the first session. (Check those that you agree upon.)

❏ PRIORITY: While you are in the course, you give the group meetings priority.

❏ PARTICIPATION: Everyone participates and no one dominates.

❏ RESPECT: Everyone is given the right to their own opinion and all questions are encouraged and respected.

❏ CONFIDENTIALITY: Anything that is said in the meeting is never repeated outside the meeting.

❏ EMPTY CHAIR: The group stays open to new people at every meeting.

❏ SUPPORT: Permission is given to call upon each other in time of need—even in the middle of the night.

❏ ADVICE GIVING: Unsolicited advice is not allowed.

❏ MISSION: We agree to do everything in our power to start a new group as our mission (see center section).

13. As a group, you may want to address the following:

• The time and place this group is going to meet
• Responsibility for refreshments
• Child care

Getting Acquainted

3-PART AGENDA

ICE-BREAKER
15 Minutes

BIBLE STUDY
30 Minutes

CARING TIME
15–45 Minutes

Welcome to this group for couples who want to make a good marriage better. Too often people pay attention to their marriage only when a serious problem develops. That is like taking your car in only when it needs to be repaired, but never for maintenance. Certainly marriage is much more valuable than a car!

Paying attention to our marriage means taking time to celebrate the good and learn from the bad. It means talking about the pressures of marriage—pressures from work, finances, schedules, in-laws, children, and grandchildren.

These pressures would be easier to handle if it weren't for the fact that we also have to adapt to each other. As soon as we think we have the other person figured out, he or she changes, and we have to readapt! Still, it is such growth and change which can bring excitement (as well as challenge) to a marriage. David and Vera Mace, authors of the book, *We Can Have Better Marriages if We Really Want Them*, write: "Marriage has too often been portrayed as two people frozen together side by side, immobile as marble statues. More accurately, it is the intricate and graceful cooperation of two dancers who have learned to match each other's movements and moods in response to the music of the spheres."

> **LEADER: Be sure to read the "Questions and Answers" on pages 3–5. Take some time during this first session to have the group go over the ground rules on page 5. At the beginning of the Caring Time have your group look at pages M1–M3 in the center section of this book.**

In this course, we will seek to learn ways to better "choreograph" that dance. We will do so by looking at our past as a couple, to celebrate and learn from the good times and the bad times. We will take time to look at our differing values and how they can enrich marriage; the extended family relationships which both enhance and challenge our union; the beauty and excitement our sexuality brings to marriage; and finally the challenge of that part of the vows that says: "till death do us part."

Every session has three parts: (1) **Ice-Breaker**—to break the ice and introduce the topic, (2) **Bible Study**—to share your life through a passage of Scripture, and (3) **Caring Time**—to share prayer concerns and pray for one another.

Ice-Breaker / 15 Minutes

First Impressions. Take a few minutes and share two or three stories of your first impressions of your spouse. If your spouse leaves out some of the juicy details to the questions below, feel free to add to their story.

1. What two adjectives describe your first impression of your spouse?

❏ ravishing	❏ bright	❏ angelic
❏ voluptuous	❏ charming	❏ effervescent
❏ sexy	❏ crazy	❏ wild
❏ gorgeous	❏ fun	❏ old-fashioned
❏ irresistible	❏ spiritual	❏ motherly
❏ virile	❏ disarming	❏ macho
❏ muscular	❏ classy	❏ pushy
❏ innocent	❏ obnoxious	❏ special

2. FIRST MEETING: Where was it? What occasion?

3. FIRST HANGOUT: Where was your favorite meeting place?

4. FIRST DATE: Where did you go? What happened?

5. FIRST KISS: Where was it?

6. FIRST CAR: What was it? Color? Condition? Cost?

7. FIRST PROPOSAL: Where? How?

8. FIRST FIGHT: What was it about?

9. FIRST SONG: What did you consider "Our Song"?

In this first session, you will have a chance to compare your wedding story to a wedding story in Scripture. Ask one person to read out loud the Scripture passage below. Then, discuss the questions that follow. Be sure to save a few minutes at the close for the Caring Time.

Bible Study / 30 Minutes

John 2:1–11 / The Wedding at Cana

2 On the third day a wedding took place at Cana in Galilee. Jesus' mother was there, ²and Jesus and his disciples had also been invited to the wedding. ³When the wine was gone, Jesus' mother said to him, "They have no more wine."

⁴"Dear woman, why do you involve me?" Jesus replied. "My time has not yet come."

⁵His mother said to his servants, "Do whatever he tells you."

⁶Nearby stood six stone water jars, the kind used by the Jews for ceremonial washing, each holding from twenty to thirty gallons.

⁷Jesus said to the servants, "Fill the jars with water"; so they filled them to the brim.

⁸Then he told them, "Now draw some out and take it to the master of the banquet."

They did so, ⁹and the master of the banquet tasted the water that had been turned into wine. He did not realize where it had come from, though the servants who had drawn the water knew. Then he called the bridegroom aside ¹⁰and said, "Everyone brings out the choice wine first and then the cheaper wine after the guests have had too much to drink; but you have saved the best till now."

¹¹This, the first of his miraculous signs, Jesus performed at Cana in Galilee. He thus revealed his glory, and his disciples put their faith in him.

1. If you could compare your wedding reception to this one, how would you do so?
   ❏ Ours was simpler.
   ❏ We didn't serve wine.
   ❏ Ours was even more chaotic.
   ❏ My mother took charge.
   ❏ It wasn't the wine, but it was the ...

2. How would you compare your marriage today to the day you were married?
❏ Well ...
❏ It's different.
❏ We've grown.
❏ We've settled down.
❏ The cork has been out of the wine bottle for a while.

3. How would you compare the way Jesus' mother acted at the wedding to the way your parents acted at your wedding?
❏ My mother acted just like Jesus' mother.
❏ My dad cried when he gave me away.
❏ We didn't have a reception.
❏ Everything went fine, until ...
❏ I don't even want to talk about it.

4. What motivated you to come to this group?
❏ I was curious.
❏ A friend asked us.
❏ I had nothing better to do.
❏ My spouse asked me.
❏ A desire to strengthen my marriage.
❏ other:_____

5. What are your expectations for this group?
❏ to get to know some other couples
❏ to relax and forget about the pressures of life for a while
❏ to see what the Bible has to say about marriage
❏ to explore healthier ways to relate to each other
❏ to "compare notes" with other couples
❏ to share in an enjoyable way with my spouse
❏ other:_____

6. How do you feel about opening up and sharing with this group?
❏ nervous
❏ Okay, but ...
❏ concerned about what my spouse might say
❏ How far is this going to go?
❏ I'm not the sharing type.

7. If you are going to belong to this group, what is one thing you want understood?
❏ Anything that is said stays in this room.
❏ I'm not the gushy type.
❏ Please don't push me.
❏ other:_____

Caring Time / 15–45 Minutes

The most important time in every meeting is this—the Caring Time—where you take time to share prayer requests and pray for one another. To make sure that this time is not neglected, you need to set a minimum time that you will devote to prayer requests and prayer and count backwards from the closing time by this amount. For instance, if you are going to close at 9 p.m., and you are going to devote 30 minutes to prayer requests and prayer, you need to ask a timekeeper to call "time" at 8:30 and move to prayer requests. Start out by asking everyone to answer this question:

"How can we help you in prayer this week?"

Then, move into prayer. If you have not prayed out loud before, finish these sentences:

"Hello, God, this is ... (first name). I want to thank you for ..."

Be sure to pray for the "empty chair." (See "empty chair" on page M5 in the center section.) Think about who you could invite to join the group as you begin this study.

LEADER: Ask the group, "Who are you going to invite for next week?"

GROUP DIRECTORY

P.S.
At the close, pass around your books and have everyone sign the Group Directory inside the front cover.

For Better or Worse

3-PART AGENDA

ICE-BREAKER
15 Minutes

BIBLE STUDY
30 Minutes

CARING TIME
15–45 Minutes

Since the time of Adam and Eve, marriages have had their ups and downs. Even though Americans have a high divorce rate, most people still want to be married. For many people, the benefits of marriage outweigh their fear of divorce.

Successful marriages take work. After the honeymoon is over, the marriage relationship must become more intentional. In the first years of marriage, couples are getting to know each other. In the middle years, the effort is put into balancing work with raising children. And after the children leave, the marriage enters the mature stage where often the relationship needs to be redefined.

But what really makes a marriage succeed? In addition to love, commitment and responsibility are necessary. When the going gets tough, as it does in all marriages, couples need to work hard to keep their union intact. Long-term successful couples never take each other for granted. Even while raising children, they realize that their first and main commitment is to being a couple.

> **LEADER:** *If there are new people in this session, review the ground rules for this group on page 5. Have the group look at page M4 in the center section and decide which Bible Study option to use—light or heavy. If you have more than seven people, see the box about the "Fearless Foursome" on page 4.*

In this session, you will have a chance to share some of your "humble beginnings" as a couple.

Starting with this session, you will be given two options for Bible Study. Option 1 is a story passage with a guided questionnaire for easy sharing. Option 2 is a passage from an epistle with deeper questions and Reference Notes about the passage. Be sure to save time at the close for the Caring Time—to share prayer requests and pray for one another.

Ice-Breaker / 15 Minutes

Home Improvement. In the Bible Study, you will have a chance to talk about the early days of your marriage. Right now, take turns answering these two questions about your present home.

1. If you had to give up one modern convenience in your home right now, what would be your first and last choices?
- ❐ indoor toilet
- ❐ electric lights
- ❐ air-conditioning
- ❐ telephone
- ❐ refrigerator
- ❐ clothes dryer
- ❐ central heat
- ❐ TV / stereo
- ❐ dishwasher
- ❐ computer

2. If you could add one luxury to your home, what would you choose?
- ❐ hot tub / pool
- ❐ video library of my favorite movies
- ❐ TV satellite dish for 24-hour sports
- ❐ massage table / sauna
- ❐ original oil painting
- ❐ pool table
- ❐ finished basement
- ❐ maid for one year
- ❐ great books library

Bible Study / 30 Minutes

Option 1 / Gospel Study

Luke 2:1–7 / Humble Beginnings

2 In those days Caesar Augustus issued a decree that a census should be taken of the entire Roman world. ²(This was the first census that took place while Quirinius was governor of Syria.) ³And everyone went to his own town to register.

⁴So Joseph also went up from the town of Nazareth in Galilee to Judea, to Bethlehem the town of David, because he belonged to the house and line of David. ⁵He went there to register with Mary, who was pledged to be married to him and was expecting a child. ⁶While they were there, the time came for the baby to be born, ⁷and she gave birth to her firstborn, a son. She wrapped him in cloths and placed him in a manger, because there was no room for them in the inn.

1. Pregnant. Broke. Homeless. What chance would you give this marriage?
   ❏ none
   ❏ uphill all the way
   ❏ fifty-fifty
   ❏ the best way to begin

2. MEN: If you had been in Joseph's shoes, what would you have done?
   ❏ copped out   ❏ become depressed
   ❏ rose to the occasion   ❏ stood by Mary
   ❏ called for help   ❏ other:_____

3. WOMEN: If you had been in Mary's shoes, what would you have done?
   ❏ withdrawn   ❏ plucked up courage
   ❏ taken it out on Joseph   ❏ other: _____
   ❏ cried a lot

4. Do you think the "humble" beginnings of this marriage were purely coincidental, or all part of the plan and purpose of God?
   ❏ It was purely coincidental.
   ❏ It was all part of the plan and purpose of God.
   ❏ "Humble" beginnings make better marriages.

5. How would their "humble" beginnings make for a better marriage?
   ❏ It caused them to grow up fast.
   ❏ It caused them to depend upon God.
   ❏ Struggling is the best teacher.

6. How would you compare your start in marriage to that of Mary and Joseph?
   ❏ At least we were not pregnant.
   ❏ At least we had a place to stay.
   ❏ We had it easier—barely.
   ❏ We had it much easier.

7. How would you feel about going back to the early days of your marriage?
   ❏ It was sure easier.
   ❏ I'm glad we started out that way, but I would not go back.
   ❏ It all depends.
   ❏ other:_____

13

8. What did you learn from the early days in your marriage that you would like to pass on to your kids concerning marriage?
- ❒ God didn't promise a rose garden.
- ❒ Struggles only deepen the relationship.
- ❒ Keep a sense of humor.
- ❒ other: ____________________

9. If you had it to do over, what is one thing you would do differently in the early days of your marriage?
- ❒ set ground rules for fighting
- ❒ define expectations more clearly
- ❒ go together for marriage counseling
- ❒ read a good book on sex
- ❒ other: ____________________

Option 2 / Epistle Study

James 1:2–12 / Hard Times

How would you like to be the pastor of a church where there was high unemployment in the region, no welfare system except your church, and many of your people on the verge of starvation? Listen as the pastor gives some advice. (The Reference Notes on pages 16–17 will help you better understand the passage.)

[2]Consider it pure joy, my brothers, whenever you face trials of many
kinds, [3]because you know that the testing of your faith develops persever-
ance. [4]Perseverance must finish its work so that you may be mature and
complete, not lacking anything. [5]If any of you lacks wisdom, he should ask
God, who gives generously to all without finding fault, and it will be given
to him. [6]But when he asks, he must believe and not doubt, because he who
doubts is like a wave of the sea, blown and tossed by the wind. [7]That man
should not think he will receive anything from the Lord; [8]he is a double-
minded man, unstable in all he does.

[9]The brother in humble circumstances ought to take pride in his high
position. [10]But the one who is rich should take pride in his low position,
because he will pass away like a wild flower. [11]For the sun rises with scorch-
ing heat and withers the plant; its blossom falls and its beauty is destroyed.
In the same way, the rich man will fade away even while he goes about his
business.

[12]Blessed is the man who perseveres under trial, because when he has stood the test, he will receive the crown of life that God has promised to those who love him.

1. Which of the following characteristics do you think are most important in making a successful marriage? (choose three)

___ integrity	___ sense of humor
___ flexibility	___ sensitivity
___ commitment	___ perseverance
___ caring	___ being friends
___ submission	___ common sense
___ understanding	___ unselfishness
___ assertiveness	___ love
___ patience	___ honesty

2. In your own marriage, what was the first real crisis you had to face and how did you deal with it?

3. What message in this passage would have helped you deal with that crisis in a better way?

4. In what ways have the hard times in your marriage brought you closer together?

5. In what ways have the hard times in your marriage brought you closer to God?

6. How would you paraphrase verse 12 in your own words?

7. What is the key verse in this passage for you? How will you apply it to your marriage?

Caring Time / 15–45 Minutes

Take time at the close to share any personal prayer requests. Answer the question:

"How can we help you in prayer this week?"

Then go around and let each person pray for the person on their right. Finish this sentence:

"Dear God, I want to speak to you about my friend _____."

1:2 *Consider it pure joy.* Christians ought to view the difficulties of life with enthusiasm, because the outcome of trials will be beneficial. The joy he is talking about is not just a feeling, however. It is a form of activity. It is active acceptance of adversity.

trials of many kinds. The word "trials" has the dual sense of "adversity" (e.g., disease, persecution, tragedy) and "temptations" (e.g., lust, greed, trust in wealth).

1:3 One reason that the Christian can rejoice in suffering is because immediate good does come out of the pain. In this verse James assumes that there will be good results.

perseverance. Or "endurance" (sticking it out). It is used in the sense of active overcoming rather than passive acceptance.

1:4 *finish its work.* Perfection is not automatic—it takes time and effort.

mature and complete. James has in mind here *wholeness of character.* He is not calling for some sort of esoteric perfection or sinlessness. Instead, the emphasis is on moral blamelessness. He is thinking of the integrated life, in contrast to the divided person of verses 6–8.

1:5–8 Wisdom is needed in order to deal with trials so that they produce wholeness of character. Wisdom is needed to understand how to consider such adversity *pure joy.*

1:5 *wisdom.* This is not just abstract knowledge, but God-given insight which issues in right living. It is the ability to make right decisions especially about moral issues, as one is called upon to do during trials.

1:6 James now contrasts the lack of hesitation on God's part to give (v. 5) with the hesitation on people's part to ask (v. 6). Both here and in James 4:3, unanswered prayer is connected to the quality of the asking, not to the unwillingness of God to give.

believe. To be in *one mind* about God's ability to answer prayer, to be sure that God will hear and will act in accord with his superior wisdom.

1:8 *double-minded.* To doubt is to be in *two minds*—to believe and to disbelieve simultaneously.

1:9–11 Poverty is an example of a trial to be endured but so too are riches, though in quite a different way.

1:9 *humble circumstances.* Those who are poor in a material and social sense, and who are looked down on by others because they are poor.

take pride. This becomes possible when the poor see beyond immediate circumstances to their new position as children of God. They may be poor in worldly goods, but they are rich beyond imagining since they are children of God, and heirs of the whole world.

high position. In the early church, the poor gained a new sense of self-respect. Slaves found that traditional social distinctions had been obliterated (Gal. 3:28).

1:10 *rich.* The peril of riches is that people come to trust in wealth as a source of security. It is a mark of double-mindedness to attempt to serve both God and money. The word "rich," in James, "always indicates one outside the community, a non-believing person. The rich, in fact, are the oppressors of the community (2:6; 5:1–6)." (Davids).

low position. Jewish culture understood wealth to be a sure sign of God's favor. Here, as elsewhere (vv. 2,9), James reverses conventional expectations.

1:12 *Blessed.* Happy is he or she who has withstood all the trials to the end.

perseveres. In verse 3, James says testing produces perseverance. Here he points out that such perseverance brings the reward of blessedness.

stood the test. Such a person is like metal which has been purged by fire and is purified of all foreign substances.

crown of life. As with Paul (Rom. 5:1–5) and Peter (1 Peter 1:6–7), James now focuses on the final result of endurance under trial: eternal life.

GROUP DIRECTORY

P.S.
If you have a new person in your group, be sure to add their name to the group directory inside the front cover.

Love, Honor, Cherish

3-PART AGENDA

ICE-BREAKER
15 Minutes

BIBLE STUDY
30 Minutes

CARING TIME
15–45 Minutes

Love, honor and cherish: These three simple words express important things we promised to do when we were married. But what do they mean? Are they just nice-sounding words we use when romance is in the air, and which we promptly forget when "the rubber hits the road" in the day-to-day issues of marriage?

There are essentially three New Testament words which can be translated into the English word "love." *Eros* means romantic or sexual love. We must never demean that kind of love as trivial, or dishonor it by relegating it to R- or X-rated movies. *Eros* was at the heart of our original attraction to each other, and it is at the heart of God's plan for life. Nevertheless, *eros* often focuses on the physical, and does not express the height of what love can be. *Phileo* is what we sometimes call "brotherly love," but it isn't necessarily gender-related. This kind of love for our spouse as a companion and fellow-traveler on life's journey is also important. But beyond this kind of love is *agape*, which is God's love. This love goes beyond our own self-focused need— it is love with no strings attached. We show this love when we stop thinking "50–50" and give of ourselves fully to the other person's need and to the needs of our marriage.

LEADER: If there are more than seven people at this meeting, divide into groups of 4 for the Bible Study. Count off around the group: "one, two, one, two, etc."—and have the "ones" quickly move to another room. When you come back together for the Caring Time, have the group read about their Mission on page M5 of the center section.

Certainly love also includes the idea of "honoring" and "cherishing" our partner. To "honor" someone is, according to Webster, to show them "high regard or respect." When we disrespect our spouse, it can lead to assaults—either verbal or physical—and this happens in too many marriages today. To "cherish" our spouse means to "hold them dear"—to value our spouse as more dear to us than professional recognition, material luxury, or any of the other things we sometimes place ahead of our marriage.

The following ice-breaker is just for fun and should not last more than 15 minutes. Be sure to save time at the close for prayer requests and prayer.

Ice-Breaker / 15 Minutes

How I See Myself. Taking one category at a time, put an *"X"* somewhere in between the two extremes to indicate how you see yourself. For instance, on MANNERS you might put the *"X"* in the middle because you are in between the two extremes.

MANNERS
Mr. / Miss Manners _____Rude Dude

FITNESS
Mr. / Miss Universe _____Couch Potato

SENSITIVITY
I'm listening _____I can't hear you

FASHION
All dressed up _____Grubbies

NEATNESS
Mr. / Miss Clean _____Mr. / Miss Messy

SEX APPEAL
Homecoming king / queen _____Kermit / Miss Piggy

ATHLETICISM
Most Valuable Player _____Bench Warmer

TALENT
Virtuoso _____Spectator

CHARM
Prince / Princess Charming _____Oscar the Grouch

Bible Study / 30 Minutes

Option 1 / Story Passage

Genesis 2:18–25 / Adam and Eve

[18]The LORD God said, "It is not good for the man to be alone. I will make a helper suitable for him."

[19]Now the LORD God had formed out of the ground all the beasts of the field and all the birds of the air. He brought them to the man to see what he would name them; and whatever the man called each living creature, that was its name. [20]So the man gave names to all the livestock, the birds of the air and all the beasts of the field.

But for Adam no suitable helper was found. [21]So the LORD God caused the man to fall into a deep sleep; and while he was sleeping, he took one of the man's ribs and closed up the place with flesh. [22]Then the LORD God made a woman from the rib he had taken out of the man, and he brought her to the man.

[23]The man said,

> *"This is now bone of my bones*
> *and flesh of my flesh;*
> *she shall be called 'woman,'*
> *for she was taken out of man."*

[24]For this reason a man will leave his father and mother and be united to his wife, and they will become one flesh.

[25]The man and his wife were both naked, and they felt no shame.

"The more that a person is able to set aside power for the sake of love, the more fully love will be expressed."
—Tony Campolo

1. What is your short definition of a good marriage?
   - ❏ spiritual teammate
   - ❏ growing old together
   - ❏ cook and bottle washer
   - ❏ a safe harbor
   - ❏ a lifetime friend
   - ❏ a fun partner

2. Who do you look up to as a role model for a good marriage?
   - ❏ my parents
   - ❏ my grandparents
   - ❏ a special couple in our church
   - ❏ my spouse's parents
   - ❏ our close friends
   - ❏ I don't know of anyone.

3. What does this story say to you about the nature of men and women?
   - ❏ Men and women need each other.
   - ❏ Men are created with unique authority and responsibility.
   - ❏ Women are designed to be helpers.
   - ❏ Men are more task-oriented and women more relational.
   - ❏ Men and women are more alike than different.

4. What do you think God meant when he referred to Eve as a "suitable helper" (v. 20)?
   ❐ She will serve Adam.
   ❐ She will be a great partner.
   ❐ She will be a source of strength.
   ❐ Adam and Eve will work together.

5. Why did God create a woman for Adam?
   ❐ sex—marital bliss
   ❐ procreation—children
   ❐ comfort from loneliness
   ❐ other: _____

6. Which of the following are you most grateful for in your marriage? Which would you like to focus on for growth?
   ❐ our mutual help and support
   ❐ the companionship we share
   ❐ the sizzle of our romance
   ❐ the intimacy of our relationship

7. What have you found is the best way to stay "united"?
   ❐ being honest about our needs
   ❐ praying together
   ❐ having fun together
   ❐ having time away from each other
   ❐ never going to bed mad

Option 2 / Epistle Study

Philippians 2:1–11 / Tough Act to Follow

If the relationship in marriage is supposed to be like the relationship between Christ and the church, it might be good to look at the attitude that Christ had in his time on earth. This is one of the most sublime passages in Scripture. After reading the passage out loud, discuss the questions that follow. (Remember to use the Reference Notes as needed for help.)

2 *If you have any encouragement from being united with Christ, if any comfort from his love, if any fellowship with the Spirit, if any tenderness and compassion, ²then make my joy complete by being like-minded, having the same love, being one in spirit and purpose. ³Do nothing out of selfish* ambition or vain conceit, but in humility consider others better than your-selves. *Each of you should look not only to your own interests, but also to the interests of others.*

Your attitude should be the same as that of Christ Jesus:

Who, being in very nature God,
did not consider equality with God something
to be grasped,
but made himself nothing,
taking the very nature of a servant,
being made in human likeness.
And being found in appearance as a man,
he humbled himself
and became obedient to death—
even death on a cross!
Therefore God exalted him to the highest place
and gave him the name that is above every
name,
that at the name of Jesus every knee should bow,
in heaven and on earth and under the earth,
and every tongue confess that Jesus Christ is Lord,
to the glory of God the Father.

1. Who takes out the trash in your home? Cleans the toilet?

2. Where in your life could you use an "attitude adjustment"?

3. Are you able to accept your spouse as they are, or are you trying to make them a little better?

4. Reading between the lines in this Scripture passage (verses 1–4), what was wrong with the church in Philippi?

5. How does this passage challenge society's definition of success? What is your definition of success?

6. What does it mean to consider someone "better than yourself"? How does humility differ from being a doormat?

7. What is one specific way you can imitate Christ's humility in the way you treat your spouse this coming week?

8. In the list below, what are two or three strengths that you bring to your marriage, and what are two or three strengths that your spouse brings to your marriage?

____ loyalty (sticking up for each other)

W__ love (warmth and affection)

____ affirmation (praise and acceptance)

W_ fun (good times as a family)

____ thoughtfulness (consideration of others)

____ togetherness (enjoy being together)

____ hospitality (can bring friends home)

____ trust (believing each other because we tell the truth)

J__ commitment (sticking together through thick and thin)

____ forgiveness (quick to say "I'm sorry")

____ sensitivity (caring)

J__ responsibility (teamwork)

W__ security (safety, sense of protection)

____ unselfishness (giving up of personal desires)

____ sense of humor (ability to laugh at our mistakes)

____ communication (with listening)

Caring Time / 15–45 Minutes

Take a few minutes at the close to share any concerns and pray for one another. Answer this question:

"How can we help you in prayer this week?"

LEADER: Ask the group, "Who are you going to invite for next week?"

Then, go around and let each person pray for the person on their right. Finish the sentence:

"Dear God, I want to speak to you about my friend _____."

Reference Notes

2:1 By means of four clauses, Paul urges the Philippians to say "Yes" to his request that they live together in harmony. They have a strong incentive to be united to one another because of their experience of the encouragement, love, fellowship, mercy and compassion of God the Father, Son and Holy Spirit.

If. In Greek, this construction assumes a positive response, e.g., "If you have any encouragement, as of course you do ..."

2:2 Paul continues to urge them to be united. In this verse, he uses four parallel clauses, each of which makes this point. He calls for them to "think the same way," to "have the same love," to be "one in soul," and finally, repeating himself, to "think the one thing." (These are literal renderings of the four Greek clauses.)

like-minded. This is literally, "think the same way." However, Paul is not just urging everyone to hold identical ideas and opinions. The word for "think" is far more comprehensive and involves not only one's mind, but one's feelings, attitudes and will. Paul is calling for a far deeper form of unity than simple doctrinal conformity.

one in spirit. In Greek, this is a single word which Paul probably made up since it is found nowhere else.

2:3–4 The road to unity is via the path of humble self-sacrifice. Paul has already demonstrated what he is urging here by means of his selfless attitude to those Christian brothers and sisters who preach Christ from false motives (see Phil. 1:18).

2:3 *selfish ambition.* This is the second time Paul has used this word (see Phil. 1:17). It means working to advance oneself without thought for others.

vain conceit. This is the only occurrence of this word in the New Testament. Translated literally, it means "vain glory" (*kenodoxia*) which is asserting oneself over God who alone is worthy of true glory (*doxa*). This is the sort of person who will arrogantly assert that they are right even though what that person holds is false. This is a person whose concern is for personal prestige.

humility. This was not a virtue that was valued by the Greeks in the first century. They considered this to be the attitude of a slave, i.e., servility. In the Old Testament, however, this was understood to be the proper attitude to hold before God. What Paul means by humility is defined by the phrase that follows. Humility is "considering others better than yourself." Christians are to accord others the same dignity and respect that Christ has given to all people. Humility involves seeing others not on the basis of how clever, attractive, or pious they are, but through the eyes of Christ who died for them.

2:4 *look not only to your own interests.* This is literally, "keeping your eye on" your own interests. Preoccupation with personal interests, along with selfish ambition and vain conceit, make unity impossible. Individualism or partisanship work against community. Note that Paul says "look *not only* to your own interests." Personal interests are important (although not to the exclusion of everything else). This is a call to love, not to masochism.

the interests of others. Instead, the Philippians should focus on the good points in others. "Rejoice in the honor paid to others rather than in that paid to yourself" (Bruce). (See also Romans 15:1–3; Galatians 6:2.)

2:5–11 From a theological point of view, this is the most important section in Philippians. Here Paul provides an amazing glimpse into the nature of Jesus Christ. Through Paul's eyes we see Jesus, the divine Savior who comes to his people in humility not in power; we see the Lord of the Universe before whom all bow choosing to die for his subjects; we see one who is in nature God, voluntarily descending to the depths (and becoming a servant) before he is lifted up to the heights (and assumes his kingship). This is a breathtaking glimpse that is made all the more astonishing because no one ever imagined that God would work his will in such a way. Who would have thought that God would act via weakness not via power?

2:5 This is the transition verse between the exhortation of 2:1–4 and the illustration of 2:6–11. In it Paul states that the model for the sort of self-sacrificing humility he has been urging is found in Jesus.

2:6–11 There is little agreement between scholars as to how this hymn breaks into verses or how it is to be phrased. However, one thing is clear. The hymn has two equal parts. Part one (vv. 6–8) focuses on the self-humiliation of Jesus. Part two (vv. 9–11) focuses on God's exaltation of Jesus. In part one, Jesus is the subject of the two main verbs, while in part two, God is the subject of the two main verbs.

2:6 *being.* This is not the normal Greek word for "being." "It describes that which a man is in his very essence, that which cannot be changed" (Barclay). This word also carries the idea of *preexistence*. By using it Paul is saying that Jesus always existed in the form of God.

very nature. The Greek word used here is *morphe* (used twice by Paul in this hymn). He says that Jesus was "in very nature God" and that he then took upon himself "the very nature of a servant." This is a key word in understanding the nature of Christ. Barclay defines *morphe* as "the essential form of something which never alters," in contrast to the word *schema* (used by Paul in v. 7), which denotes outward and changeable forms. In other words, Jesus possessed the essential nature of God. Why

25

doesn't he say this more directly? In the same way that a Jew could not bring himself to pronounce the name of God, a strict monotheist like Paul cannot quite bring himself to say bluntly: "Jesus is God," though he ends up saying this very thing.

to be grasped. This is another rare word, used only at this point in the New Testament. It refers to the fact that Jesus did not have to "snatch" equality with God. Equality was not something he needed to acquire. It was his already, and thus he could give it away. Giving, not grasping, is what Jesus did.

2:7–8 Paul uses four phrases to define what happened in the Incarnation. Jesus "made himself nothing"; he took "the very nature of a servant"; he was made "in human likeness"; and he was "found in appearance as a man." Each phrase gives a different glimpse into what Jesus became.

2:7 made himself nothing. Instead of grasping Godhood, Christ gave away what he had. This word means, literally, "to empty," or "to pour out until the container is empty." The way this is phrased indicates that this is something which Christ did voluntarily.

taking the very nature of a servant. Jesus gave up Godhood and took on slavehood. From being the ultimate master, he became the lowest servant. He left ruling for serving. *Morphe* is used here again, indicating that Jesus adopted the essential nature of a slave. He did not "play act" being a slave for a time. The use of the word "slave" here "emphasizes the fact that in the incarnation Christ entered the stream of human life as a slave, that is, as a person without advantage, with no rights or privileges of his own for the express purpose of placing himself completely at the service of all mankind" (Hawthorne).

being made. In contrast to the verb in verse 6 (which stresses Christ's *eternal* nature), this verb points to the fact that at a particular time he was born in the likeness of a human being.

human likeness. The point is not that Jesus just seemed to be human. He assumed the identity of a person and was similar in all ways to other human beings.

2:8 in appearance as a man. The word translated "in appearance" is *schema,* and denotes that which is outward and changeable (over against *morphe,* which denotes that which is essential and eternal). In other words, Jesus was a true man, but only temporarily. As Barclay puts it: "He is essentially divine; but he was for a time human. His mankind was utterly real, but it was something which passed: the godhead was also utterly real, but it is something which abides forever."

he humbled himself. This is the central point that Paul wants to make. This is why he offered this illustration. Jesus is the ultimate model of one who lived a life of self-sacrifice, self-renunciation, and self-surrender. Jesus existed at the pinnacle and yet descended to the very base. There has never been a more radical humbling. Furthermore, this was not something forced upon Jesus. This was voluntarily chosen by Christ. It was not compelled by circumstances.

obedient to death. The extent of this humbling is defined by this clause. Jesus humbled himself to the furthest point one can go. He submitted to death itself for the sake of both God and humanity. There was no more dramatic way to demonstrate humility.

death on a cross. This was no ordinary death. For one thing, it came about in an unusually cruel way. Crucifixion was a harsh, demeaning and utterly painful way to die. For another thing, according to the Old Testament, those who died by hanging on a tree were considered to have been cursed by God (See Deut. 21:22–23; 1 Cor. 1:23; Gal. 3:13). For a Jew there was no more humiliating way to die. Jesus, who was equal to God, died like an accursed criminal. His descent from glory had brought him as low as one could go.

2:10 Jesus. It is significant that the one before whom all will bow is Jesus, the man from Nazareth. The cosmic Lord is none other than the person who walked the roads of Palestine and talked to the people of Israel. He had a hometown, a family, a trade, and disciples. The one before whom Christians will stand at the Last Judgment is not an anonymous Life Force, but the man of Galilee who has a familiar face.

bow. Everyone will one day pay homage to Jesus. This worship will come from all of creation—all angels (in heaven), all people (on earth), and all demons (under the earth).

2:11 Jesus Christ is Lord. The climax of this hymn. This is the earliest and most basic confession of faith on the part of the church (see Acts 2:36; Rom. 10:9; 1 Cor. 12:3).

Lord. This is the name that was given to Jesus; the name that reflects who he really is (see v. 9). This is the name of God. Jesus is the supreme Sovereign of the unvierse.

Please Pass the Roles

3-PART AGENDA

ICE-BREAKER
15 Minutes

BIBLE STUDY
30 Minutes

CARING TIME
15–45 Minutes

More and more "experts" are affirming what many of us have known all along—there are definite differences between men and women! Christian marriage counselor H. Norman Wright says in his book *Romancing Your Marriage*: "You married a foreigner! You may have married someone of the same race or nationality, but you each were raised in a different culture." That's true! And that "different culture" has different values. Marriage therapist John Gray writes in his book *Men Are From Mars, Women Are From Venus* that men (Martians) value power, competency, efficiency, and achievement; while women (Venusians) value love, communication, beauty, and relationships.

The question is this: How do we respond to these differences between men and women? Some fight them every step of the way. Women try to make men think and act more like women, and men try to make women think and act more like men. This is when we need to remember the French phrase—*Vive la Difference!* That phrase essentially means, "long live the differences" between men and women. The key, then, is seeing what our spouse values, and then appreciating and respecting the fact that we are different. If we were all the same, what would we contribute to each other? What could we bring to the other person to help them to become more complete?

LEADER: If you have a new person at this session, remember to use Option 1 rather than Option 2 for the Bible Study. During the Caring Time, don't forget to keep praying for the empty chair.

In the last session, you had a chance to consider your differences and to look at the model of Christ who "emptied himself" for his bride, the church. In this session, you will go a little further and discuss the roles you play in your marriage. Be sure to save time at the close for prayer requests and prayer.

Ice-Breaker / 15 Minutes

My Romantic Scenario. Describe your perfect romantic day by finishing the sentences below. In this fantasy, money is no object, so let your imagination run wild! Instead of taking one question at a time, have each person share their complete scenario before going on to the next person.

1. "For my perfect romantic day we would travel by Lear jet to ..."
   - ❏ Paris
   - ❏ Rome
   - ❏ San Francisco
   - ❏ Maui
   - ❏ the outback of Australia
   - ❏ Puerto Vallarta
   - ❏ our own little island
   - ❏ Venice
   - ❏ New York
   - ❏ Honolulu
   - ❏ Switzerland
   - ❏ Vail
   - ❏ other:_____

2. "We would spend the day ..."
   - ❏ playing on a beach
   - ❏ talking and walking hand in hand
   - ❏ shopping and exploring
   - ❏ in recreational pursuits, like skiing
   - ❏ meeting new people
   - ❏ sipping cold drinks under a parasol
   - ❏ other:_____

3. "At dinner I would have (singer's name) flown in to sing (a favorite song) just for us."

4. "We would top off the evening by ..."
   - ❏ dancing all night
   - ❏ taking a walk under the stars
   - ❏ going to a special concert
   - ❏ "turning in" early
   - ❏ other:_____

Bible Study / 30 Minutes

Option 1 / Gospel Study

John 13:1–17 / The Jesus Model

13 *It was just before the Passover Feast. Jesus knew that the time had come for him to leave this world and go to the Father. Having loved his own who were in the world, he now showed them the full extent of his love.*

²The evening meal was being served, and the devil had already prompted Judas Iscariot, son of Simon, to betray Jesus. ³Jesus knew that the Father had put all things under his power, and that he had come from God and was returning to God; ⁴so he got up from the meal, took off his outer clothing, and wrapped a towel around his waist. ⁵After that, he poured water into a basin and began to wash his disciples' feet, drying them with the towel that was wrapped around him.

⁶He came to Simon Peter, who said to him, "Lord, are you going to wash my feet?"

⁷Jesus replied, "You do not realize now what I am doing, but later you will understand."

⁸"No," said Peter, "you shall never wash my feet."

Jesus answered, "Unless I wash you, you have no part with me."

⁹"Then, Lord," Simon Peter replied, "not just my feet but my hands and my head as well!"

¹⁰Jesus answered, "A person who has had a bath needs only to wash his feet; his whole body is clean. And you are clean, though not every one of you." ¹¹For he knew who was going to betray him, and that was why he said not every one was clean.

¹²When he had finished washing their feet, he put on his clothes and returned to his place. "Do you understand what I have done for you?" he asked them. ¹³"You call me 'Teacher' and 'Lord,' and rightly so, for that is what I am. ¹⁴Now that I, your Lord and Teacher, have washed your feet, you also should wash one another's feet. ¹⁵I have set you an example that you should do as I have done for you. ¹⁶I tell you the truth, no servant is greater than his master, nor is a messenger greater than the one who sent him. ¹⁷Now that you know these things, you will be blessed if you do them."

1. What is your first impression of this story about footwashing?
- ❏ Oh, no, what are we going to talk about?
- ❏ What has this got to do with marriage?
- ❏ This practice is out-of-date.
- ❏ This is a model for any culture.

2. Why do you think Jesus washed the disciples' feet?
- ❏ to illustrate his whole mission
- ❏ to show them what love is all about
- ❏ to be an example of servanthood
- ❏ to show them real leadership

3. What would you have done if you had been there and Jesus started to wash your feet?
- ❏ left the room
- ❏ refused to let him
- ❏ broken down and cried
- ❏ felt honored by his caring act
- ❏ sat there—feeling guilty and unworthy
- ❏ jumped up and tried to wash *his* feet

4. In your spiritual life, who is the one person outside of your spouse who has demonstrated what it means to wash feet?

5. What would it mean to practice footwashing in your marriage relationship?
- ❏ to serve my spouse more
- ❏ to let my spouse serve me
- ❏ to listen to my spouse more
- ❏ to show more affection
- ❏ to show more appreciation
- ❏ to do things that aren't "my job"
- ❏ to be more patient and forgiving
- ❏ to serve with no strings attached
- ❏ to work at sharing unpleasant tasks

6. If your spouse could minister to your deepest need in the same way as Jesus ministered to the needs of his disciples, how could your spouse show their concern?

7. What's holding you back from living a life of service like Jesus demonstrated and taught?
- ❏ I might be taken advantage of.
- ❏ I don't have time.
- ❏ I guess I'm too selfish.
- ❏ I haven't had many good role models.
- ❏ Nothing really—I'm doing my best.
- ❏ other:_____

8. What would it take for your group to get into the footwashing business for other couples in your church?
- ❏ more time than we are willing to give
- ❏ a little more commitment than I am ready for
- ❏ very little—just a way to get started
- ❏ I'll have to think about this.
- ❏ other:_____

Eph. 5:21–33 / Submit One to Another

²¹Submit to one another out of reverence for Christ.

²²Wives, submit to your husbands as to the Lord. ²³For the husband is the head of the wife as Christ is the head of the church, his body, of which he is the Savior. ²⁴Now as the church submits to Christ, so also wives should submit to their husbands in everything.

²⁵Husbands, love your wives, just as Christ loved the church and gave himself up for her ²⁶to make her holy, cleansing her by the washing with water through the word, ²⁷and to present her to himself as a radiant church, without stain or wrinkle or any other blemish, but holy and blameless. ²⁸In this same way, husbands ought to love their wives as their own bodies. He who loves his wife loves himself. ²⁹After all, no one ever hated his own body, but he feeds and cares for it, just as Christ does the church—³⁰for we are members of his body. ³¹"For this reason a man will leave his father and mother and be united to his wife, and the two will become one flesh." ³²This is a profound mystery—but I am talking about Christ and the church. ³³However, each one of you also must love his wife as he loves himself, and the wife must respect her husband.

> *"We mistakenly assume that if our partners love us they will react and behave in certain ways—the ways we react and behave when we love someone. This attitude sets us up to be disappointed again and again and prevents us from taking the necessary time to communicate lovingly about our differences."*
> —John Gray

1. Which of these TV families do you most readily identify with and why?

   ___ Cleavers (*Leave It to Beaver*)   ___ Simpsons
   ___ Buckmans (*Mad About You*)   ___ Waltons
   ___ Taylors (*Home Improvement*)   ___ Jeffersons
   ___ Huxtables (*Cosby Show*)   ___ Bradys
   ___ the Addams Family   ___ other:_____

2. What would it have meant for your favorite TV couple to "submit to one another"? What does it mean for you to do this?

3. What part does our relationship with Christ play in "mutual submission" in marriage?

4. In what ways is the marriage relationship symbolic of Christ's relationship with the church?

5. Does society's emphasis on equality in marriage conflict with these verses? If so, how? If not, why not?

Leadership Training Supplement

YOU ARE
HERE

BIRTH	GROWTH	RELEASE

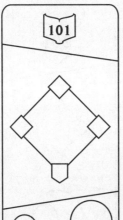

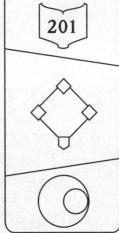

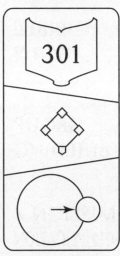

What is the game plan for your group in the 101 stage?

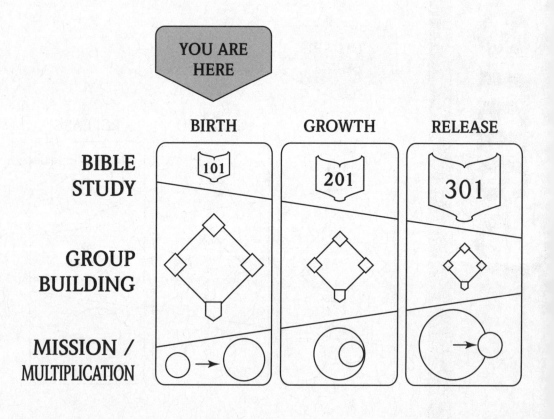

YOU ARE HERE

	BIRTH	GROWTH	RELEASE
BIBLE STUDY	101	201	301
GROUP BUILDING			
MISSION / MULTIPLICATION			

The 3-Legged Stool

The three essentials in a healthy small group are Bible Study, Group Building and Mission / Multiplication. You need all three to stay balanced—like a 3-legged stool.
- To focus only on Bible Study will lead to scholasticism.
- To focus only on Group Building will lead to narcissism.
- To focus only on Mission will lead to burnout.

You need a game plan for the life cycle of the group where all three of these elements are present in a mission-driven strategy. In the first stage of the group, here is the game plan.

Bible Study

To share your spiritual story through Scripture.

The greatest gift you can give a group is the gift of your spiritual story—the story of your spiritual beginnings, your spiritual growing pains, struggles, hopes and fears. The Bible Study is designed to help you tell your spiritual story to the group.

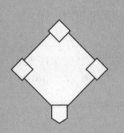

Group Building

To become a caring community.

In the first stage of a group, note how the baseball diamond is larger than the book and the circles. This is because Group Building is the priority in the first stage. Group Building is a four-step process to become a close-knit group. Using the baseball diamond illustration, the goal of Group Building—bonding—is home plate. But to get there you have to go around the bases.

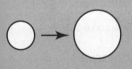

Mission / Multiplication

To grow your group numerically and spiritually.

The mission of your group is the greatest mission anyone can give their life to—to bring new people into a personal relationship with Christ and the fellowship of a Christian community. This purpose will become more prominent in the second and third stages of your group. In this stage, the goal is to invite new people into your group and try to double.

Bible Study

In the first stage of a group, the Bible Study is where you get to know each other and share your spiritual stories. The Bible Study is designed to give the leader the option of going LIGHT or HEAVY, depending on the background of the people in the group. TRACK 1 is especially designed for beginner groups who do not know a lot about the Bible or each other. TRACK 2 is for groups who are familiar with the Bible and with one another.

Track 1

Relational Bible Study (Stories)

Designed around a guided questionnaire, the questions move across the Disclosure Scale from "no risk" questions about people in the Bible story to "high risk" questions about your own life and how you would react in that situation. "If you had been in the story ..." or "the person in the story like me is ... ." The questions are open-ended—with multiple-choice options and no right or wrong answers. A person with no background knowledge of the Bible may actually have the advantage because the questions are based on first impressions.

$\longrightarrow$

The STORY in Scripture	GUIDED QUESTIONNAIRE 1 2 3 4 5 6 7 8	My STORY compared

TRACK 1: Light RELATIONAL BIBLE STUDY	TRACK 2: Heavy INDUCTIVE BIBLE STUDY
• Based on Bible stories • Open-ended questions • To share your spiritual story	• Based on Bible teachings • With observation questions • To dig into Scripture

Track 2

Inductive Bible Study (Teachings)

For groups who know each other, TRACK 2 gives you the option to go deeper in Bible Study, with questions about the text on three levels:

- Observation: What is the text saying?
- Interpretation: What does it mean?
- Application: What are you going to do about it?

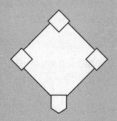

Group Building

The Baseball Diamond illustrates the four-step sharing process in bonding to become a group: (1) input; (2) feedback; (3) deeper input; and (4) deeper feedback. This process is carefully structured into the seven sessions of this course, as follows:

 Sharing My Story. My religious background. My early years and where I am right now in my spiritual journey.

 Affirming Each Other's Story. "Thank you for sharing ..." "Your story became a gift to me ..." "Your story helps me to understand where you are coming from ..."

 Sharing My Needs. "This is where I'm struggling and hurting. This is where I need to go—what I need to do."

 Caring for One Another. "How can we help you in prayer this week?" Ministry occurs as the group members serve one another through the Holy Spirit.

Mission / Multiplication

To prove that your group is "Mission-Driven," now is the time to start praying for your new "baby"—a new group to be born in the future. This is the MISSION of your group.

The birthing process begins by growing your group to about 10 or 12 people. Here are three suggestions to help your group stay focused on your Mission:

1. **Empty Chair.** Pull up an empty chair at the Caring Time and ask God to fill this chair at the next meeting.

2. **Refrigerator List.** Jot down the names of people you are going to invite and put this list on the refrigerator.

3. **New Member Home.** Move to the home of the newest member—where their friends will feel comfortable when they come to the group. On the next page, some of your questions about bringing new people into your group are answered.

Leadership Training

What if a new person joins the group in the third or fourth session?

Call the "Option Play" and go back to an EASY Bible Study that allows this person to "share their story" and get to know the people in the group.

What do you do when the group gets too large for sharing?

Take advantage of the three-part agenda and subdivide into groups of four for the Bible Study time. Count off around the group: "one, two, one, two"—and have the "ones" move quickly to another room for sharing.

What is the long-term expectation of the group for mission?

To grow the size of the group and eventually start a new group after one or two years.

What do you do when the group does not want to multiply?

This is the reason why this MISSION needs to be discussed at the beginning of a group—not at the end. If the group is committed to this MISSION at the outset, and works on this mission in stage one, they will be ready for multiplication at the end of the final stage.

What are the principles behind the Serendipity approach to Bible Study for a beginner group?

1. *Level the Playing Field.* Start the sharing with things that are easy to talk about and where everyone is equal—things that are instantly recallable—light, mischieviously revealing and childlike. Meet at the human side before moving into spiritual things.

2. *Share Your Spiritual Story.* Group Building, especially for new groups, is essential. It is crucial for Bible Study in beginner groups to help the group become a community by giving everyone the opportunity to share their spiritual history.

3. *Open Questions / Right Brain.* Open-ended questions are better than closed questions. Open questions allow for options, observations and a variety of opinions in which no one is right or wrong. Similarly, "right-brained" questions are

better than "left-brained" questions. Right-brained questions seek out your first impressions, tone, motives and subjective feelings about the text. Right-brained questions work well with narratives. Multiple-choice questionnaires encourage people who know very little about the Bible. Given a set of multiple-choice options, a new believer is not threatened, and a shy person is not intimidated. Everyone has something to contribute.

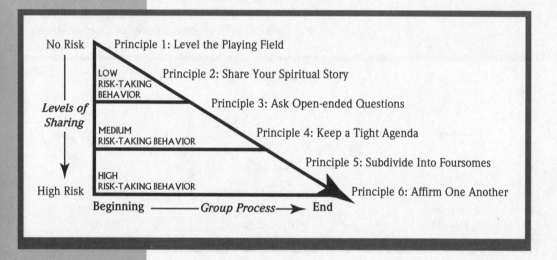

No Risk — Principle 1: Level the Playing Field

LOW RISK-TAKING BEHAVIOR — Principle 2: Share Your Spiritual Story

Principle 3: Ask Open-ended Questions

Levels of Sharing

MEDIUM RISK-TAKING BEHAVIOR — Principle 4: Keep a Tight Agenda

Principle 5: Subdivide Into Foursomes

HIGH RISK-TAKING BEHAVIOR

High Risk — Principle 6: Affirm One Another

Beginning —— *Group Process* → **End**

4. ***Tight Agenda.*** A tight agenda is better than a loose agenda for beginning small groups. Those people who might be nervous about "sharing" will find comfort knowing that the meeting agenda has been carefully organized. The more structure the first few meetings have the better, especially for a new group. Some people are afraid that a structured agenda will limit discussion. In fact, the opposite is true. The Serendipity agenda is designed to keep the discussion focused on what's important and to bring out genuine feelings, issues, and areas of need. If the goal is to move the group toward deeper relationships and a deeper experience of God, then a structured agenda is the best way to achieve that goal.

5. ***Fearless Foursomes.*** Dividing your small group into foursomes during the Bible Study can be a good idea. In groups of four, everyone will have an opportunity to participate and you can finish the Bible Study in 30 minutes. In groups of eight or more, the Bible Study will need to be longer and you will take away from the Caring Time.

Also, by subdividing into groups of four for the Bible Study time, you give others a chance to develop their skills at leading a group—in preparation for the day when you develop a small cell to eventually move out and birth a new group.

6. *Affirm the person and their story.* Give positive feedback to group members: "Thank you for sharing ... your story really helps me to understand where you are coming from ... your story was a real gift to me ... " This affirmation given honestly and genuinely will create the atmosphere for deeper sharing.

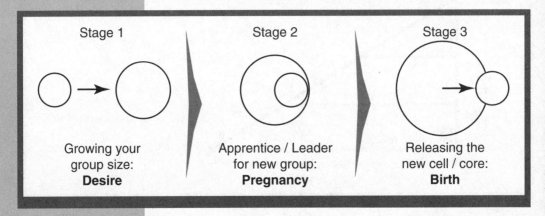

Stage 1	Stage 2	Stage 3
Growing your group size: **Desire**	Apprentice / Leader for new group: **Pregnancy**	Releasing the new cell / core: **Birth**

What is the next stage of our group all about?

In the next stage, the 201 BIBLE STUDY is deeper, GROUP BUILDING focuses on developing your gifts, and in the MISSION you will identify an Apprentice / Leader and two others within your group who will eventually become the leadership core of a new group down the road a bit.

6. In what practical ways are submission and love related in a Christian marriage? What part, if any, does "self-love" play in a marriage relationship?

7. In your own words, how would you explain the main goal of a Christian marriage?

8. What can you take from this passage that will help you be a better spouse?

Caring Time / 15–45 Minutes

LEADER: Ask the group, "Who are you going to invite for next week?"

Affirmation. Have one person sit in silence (someone who has really opened up and shared their story), and let the others in the group finish one of the sentences below and explain.

"The thing I appreciate about you is ..."

OR

"The gift that you gave to me in sharing your need was ..."

When you have finished with the first person, move on to another person, and repeat the process.

Prayer Requests and Prayer. Take time to let anyone share a prayer request and close in prayer for each other. Answer the question:

"How can we help you in prayer?"

Reference Notes

5:21 The verb in 5:21 ("submit") is linked grammatically both backward to 5:18 and forward to 5:22. Looking backward, "submit" is the last of four present participles which describe what is involved in being filled with the Spirit. Looking forward, "submit" provides the verb for 5:22, which has no verb of its own.

5:22–24 Paul first spells out what "mutual submission" means for wives.

5:22 *Wives.* In a radical departure from tradition, Paul addresses women in their own right as individuals able to make their own choices. He does not address them through their husbands (as would have been common in the first century). He does not tell husbands: "Make your wives submit to you." Rather, he speaks to wives on the same level as he will speak to husbands.

submit. This injunction from Paul must be understood in its historical context. In Jewish law, a woman was a "thing," not a person, and she had no legal rights. In describing the Greek world, Demosthenes wrote: "We have courtesans for our pleasure, prostitutes for daily physical use, wives to bring up legitimate children." In Rome, too, divorce was easy and women were repressed. Against this, Paul proposes a radical, liberating view: (1) submission was to be mutual (the man was no longer the absolute authority); (2) wives are called upon to defer only to their husbands (and not to every man); and (3) submission is defined and qualified by Christ's headship of the church (Christ died for the church). Therefore, what wives are called to submit to ("yield to," "adapt to," or "give way to") is sacrificial love! Love, not control, is the issue. "Submission is something quite different from obedience. It is a voluntary self-giving to a lover whose responsibility is defined in terms of constructive care; it is love's response to love" (Stott).

to your husbands. A woman owes submission only to her husband, not to all men (as first-century culture taught). Furthermore, "the restrictive term (lit.) 'to your own husbands' makes the wife's subordination resemble the 'yielding' which a senator gladly offers to a fellow senator, but not to any government spokesman or other interlocutor" (Barth).

5:23 *Christ is the head of the church.* Paul has already described in Ephesians 4:15–16 the way in which Christ is the head of the church. He is head in that the rest of the body derives from him the health and strength which allows each part to play its own distinctive role. It is a headship of love, not of control; of nurture, not of suppression. The word "head" when used today has the sense of "ruler" or "authority." However, in Greek, when "head" is used in a metaphorical sense as it is here, it means "origin" as in the source (head) of a river. Woman has her origins in man (see Gen. 2:18–23) just as the church has its origins in Christ. Had Paul wanted to convey the idea that the husband "rules over" the wife (as Christ "rules over" the church) he would have used a different Greek word for "head."

the Savior. The emphasis in this analogy is not on Christ as Lord but on Christ as Savior. Paul is not saying that husbands are to express "headship" via the exertion of some sort of authority (as befits a "lord"), but via the expression of sacrificial love (as characterized by the Savior).

5:25–33 Having addressed the role of wives in three verses, Paul now devotes nine verses to explain to men what mutual submission means for them.

5:25 *love your wives.* This is the main point Paul makes to husbands. It is so important that he repeats this injunction three times (vv. 25,28,33). Love is what the husband gives by way of his part in the mutual submission paradigm. This attitude stands in contrast to Jewish teaching. "The rabbis asserted that money, the contract, and intercourse make marriage. When they enumerated what else a man 'owed' to his wife, they seldom mentioned love" (Barth). As for Greek culture, although certain philosophers such as Aristotle taught that men ought to love their wives, they used a mild word for love (*phileo*) signifying the sort of affection a person has for family. Here, however, Paul urges a far stronger type of love: *agape*, which is characterized by sacrificial, self-giving action. *Agape* love is not primarily an emotion. Rather, it shows itself in concrete action rendered on behalf of the other. However, as Barth cautions, "the employment of the term 'love' to describe the marital relation does not exclude from *agape* all elements of mutual help, partnership between equals, passionate desire and sexual fulfillment."

just as Christ loved the church and gave himself up for her. Paul now makes quite clear in what sense he is speaking of Christ as head over the church. Two actions characterize Christ's role for the church: love and sacrifice. The husband is called upon to act toward his wife in the same way—that is, to die for her! (This is how Christ "gave himself up for the church.") A wife is asked to "submit" not to "authority" but to "sacrificial love."

5:25–27 *loved / gave himself up / make her holy / cleansing / present.* "These five verbs, probably from an ancient Christian hymn, describe the unfolding stages of Christ's commitment to his bride" (Stott). In comparing the marriage relationship to the relationship between Christ and the church, Paul is following a long tradition in Scripture. The Old Testament often pictured God's relationship to his people in terms of a marriage covenant (Isa. 54:4–6; Jer. 2:1–3; 31:31–32; Hos. 1:3). In the New Testament, Christ is seen as the bridegroom (Mark 2:19–20; John 3:29).

5:26 *the washing with water.* The reference is to the bridal bath prior to the wedding that was the custom of both Jews and Greeks. The action in view here is Christian baptism.

5:27 The effect of Jesus' love on the church is described here by means of three graphic images.

to present her. At a Jewish wedding the bride was presented to the groom by a friend. This was understood as a sacred duty because it was first performed by God when he brought Eve to Adam (Gen. 2:22). In this case, Jesus is both he who presents and he who receives the bride.

radiant. The word in Greek is *endoxos* and can also be translated "resplendent" or "glorious." On one level it refers to the beautiful garments worn by the bride. On another level, this word is derived from *doxa*, which refers to the very radiance of God himself. The church, his bride, has about her the aura of God (as did Moses when he came off Mount Sinai— Exodus 34:29–35), a gift given her by the bridegroom.

without stain or wrinkle. The bridegroom has removed any trace of disease (pox marks or leprosy), disfigurement or neglect.

5:28–31 In describing how husbands are to love their wives, Paul turns from the rather exalted vision of Christ's love for the church to the more mundane (but eminently realistic) level of the husband's love for himself.

5:28 *their own bodies.* The deep-rooted instinct to care for and protect oneself is to be carried over to the wife (who, through sexual intercourse, has become one flesh with her husband).

5:31 *one flesh.* Paul does not view marriage as some sort of spiritual covenant devoid of sexuality. His second illustration of how a husband is to love his wife (vv. 28–31) revolves around their sexual union, as is made explicit here by his quotation of Genesis 2:24.

5:33 *as he loves himself.* In Leviticus 19:18, the Israelites are called upon to "love your neighbor as yourself." The gauge by which they will know if they are, indeed, loving others properly is self-love: "Is this how I want to be loved?" Husbands, according to Paul, can use this same gauge for measuring their love for their wives.

respect. This means to honor and build up another person.

Baby Makes Three

3-PART AGENDA

ICE-BREAKER
15 Minutes

BIBLE STUDY
30 Minutes

CARING TIME
15–45 Minutes

Having a child is one thing; raising a child is quite another. While parenting is one of the most difficult challenges of human experience, it can also be one of the most rewarding.

Today, many parents feel ambivalent about raising children. The demands of a job or career can place excessive stress and pressure on couples and single parents who want to be conscientious in raising their children. In fact, studies have shown that most mothers work because they have to—they feel like they don't have a choice. About half of these working mothers feel cheated because they are missing out on the best years of their kids' lives. It is little wonder that many young couples have chosen to have fewer children or no children at all.

LEADER: If you haven't already, now is the time to start thinking about the next step for your group. Take a look at the 201 courses (the second stage in the small group life cycle) on the inside of the back cover.

Despite the many obstacles in parenting, many families today are thriving. In his book, *Secrets of Strong Families,* Nick Stinnett explains there are six qualities which are consistently found in strong families. They are:

• Commitment: "They have a sense of being a team."

• Appreciation: "These folks help each other feel good about themselves."

• Communication: "They spend a lot of time talking and listening."

• Time Together: "These families eat, work, play and talk together."

• Spiritual Health: "It is a unifying force that enables them to reach out in love and compassion to others."

• Coping Skills: "Some of their coping skills are seeing something positive in the crises, pulling together, being flexible, drawing on spiritual and communication strengths, and getting help from friends and professionals."

Much of the practical framework for loving, effective parenting comes from the Bible. In the following Gospel Study, we will see that Mary and Joseph had some typical parenting problems and concerns with Jesus. While Jesus was not really a typical child, we can learn from his parents' actions. We can also glean some parenting wisdom from Paul's teachings in the Ephesians passage in the Epistle Study.

Ice-Breaker / 15 Minutes

Great American Blush Awards. Imagine your group is in charge of giving an award for the most embarrassing thing a child has done to their parents. Instead of an "Emmy" we can call it a "Ruddy." Find out who in your group has had a child do the following. Then, vote on which is the most embarrassing. Give that person (or persons) the "Ruddy."

- had a child share an embarrassing family incident during the children's sermon
- had a child repeat a less-than-flattering remark you had made about someone
- had an older child dress oddly when company came over
- as a single parent, had a child propose to your date for you
- had a child bring out embarrassing hygiene products for company
- had a child publicly contradict your "little white lie"
- had a little girl lift her dress during a public function
- had a child repeat a "four-letter word" with others asking where they learned it
- had a little child shout during a quiet moment of worship, "I have to go potty!"

Bible Study / 30 Minutes

Option 1 / Gospel Study

Luke 2:41–52 / The Trip That Was

⁴¹Every year his parents went to Jerusalem for the Feast of the Passover. ⁴²When he was twelve years old, they went up to the Feast, according to the custom. ⁴³After the Feast was over, while his parents were returning home, the boy Jesus stayed behind in Jerusalem, but they were unaware of it.

⁴⁴Thinking he was in their company, they traveled on for a day. Then they began looking for him among their relatives and friends. ⁴⁵When they did not find him, they went back to Jerusalem to look for him. ⁴⁶After three days they found him in the temple courts, sitting among the teachers, listening to them and asking them questions. ⁴⁷Everyone who heard him was amazed at his understanding and his answers. ⁴⁸When his parents saw him, they were astonished. His mother said to him, "Son, why have you treated us like this? Your father and I have been anxiously searching for you."

⁴⁹"Why were you searching for me?" he asked. "Didn't you know I had to be in my Father's house?" ⁵⁰But they did not understand what he was saying to them.

⁵¹Then he went down to Nazareth with them and was obedient to them. But his mother treasured all these things in her heart. ⁵²And Jesus grew in wisdom and stature, and in favor with God and men.

1. From reading this story, what first impression do you get of the parenting style of Joseph and Mary?
   ❏ They were not very vigilant.
   ❏ They put a lot of trust in Jesus.
   ❏ They gave Jesus more freedom than parents can in today's world.
   ❏ Mary seemed to take the lead in parenting.
   ❏ They held their composure well under the circumstances.
   ❏ They reacted pretty much like most parents would have.

2. Why do you think this story was included in the Bible?
   ❏ to show that Jesus always had an interest in Scripture and God
   ❏ to show parents of every era that even Jesus gave his parents gray hair
   ❏ to give an example of controlling your temper in a tough situation
   ❏ to show that Jesus had a religious upbringing

3. What changes in Jesus does this story seem to best signal?
   ❏ a change from the perspective of a child to the perspective of an adult
   ❏ a change from an obedient attitude to a rebellious one
   ❏ a change from dependence to independence
   ❏ a change in who he thought of as "parent"
   ❏ a change from parental direction to self-direction

4. Had you been one of Jesus' parents, how would you have reacted when you discovered Jesus missing?
   ❏ called 911   ❏ gone into shock
   ❏ yelled and screamed   ❏ cried and panicked
   ❏ blamed my spouse   ❏ figured he would show up

5. How would you have reacted when you finally found Jesus in the temple courts three days later?
   ❐ cried and given him a big hug
   ❐ yelled and screamed at him
   ❐ felt confused as to what he meant
   ❐ just felt relieved the incident was over
   ❐ gently rebuked him, as Mary did
   ❐ grounded him for 1,589 weeks!
   ❐ listened to his explanation

6. When, as an adolescent, do you remember "nearly giving your parents a heart attack" as Jesus did in this story?

7. What incident does this remind you of in relation to your own kids?

8. How does this story give you comfort or insight?
   ❐ Even Jesus' parents had to go through stress and challenges.
   ❐ Even Jesus did things that disturbed his parents.
   ❐ Developing independence is necessary in growing up.
   ❐ Sometimes we misjudge children.
   ❐ Sometimes children mature without us really noticing.

9. How can you help your child to "grow in wisdom" and in their relationships in such a way that will eventually help them to be independent?

Ephesians 6:1–9 /Children, Obey Your Parents

6 *Children, obey your parents in the Lord, for this is right. ²"Honor your father and mother"—which is the first commandment with a promise— ³"that it may go well with you and that you may enjoy long life on the earth."*

⁴Fathers, do not exasperate your children; instead, bring them up in the training and instruction of the Lord.

⁵Slaves, obey your earthly masters with respect and fear, and with sincerity of heart, just as you would obey Christ. ⁶Obey them not only to win their favor when their eye is on you, but like slaves of Christ, doing the will of God from your heart. ⁷Serve wholeheartedly, as if you were serving the Lord, not men, ⁸because you know that the Lord will reward everyone for whatever good he does, whether he is slave or free.

⁹And masters, treat your slaves in the same way. Do not threaten them, since you know that he who is both their Master and yours is in heaven, and there is no favoritism with him.

"All happy families resemble one another, but each unhappy family is unhappy in its own way."
—Leo Tolstoy

1. Was obeying your parents ever a problem for you? For your children? How do you get your children to mind without losing yours?

2. According to Paul, why should children obey their parents?

3. Does this mean children should do everything their parents tell them? Why or why not?

4. In what practical ways can we "honor" our parents?

5. How can fathers "exasperate" their children?

6. How can parents raise their children "in the training and instruction of the Lord"?

7. What are the similarities and dissimilarities in the relationships of slaves to masters and children to parents?

8. How can we avoid favoritism when raising children? Does that mean treating all our children the same? Why or why not?

9. What one area of your relationship with your child(ren) needs improvement?

Caring Time / 15–45 Minutes

Take a few minutes at the close to share any concerns and pray for one another. Answer this question:

"How can we help you in prayer this week?"

LEADER:
Ask the
group, "Who
are you going
to invite for
next week?"

Then, go around and let each person pray for the person on their right. Finish the sentence:

"Dear God, I want to speak to you about my friend _____."

Reference Notes

Summary. Paul continues his discussion of the three basic sets of relationships which dominate most people's lives. Here he deals with relationships within a family (between parents and children) and the relationship between slaves and masters. Paul begins by urging children to "obey," and then gives four reasons for such obedience: (1) they are "in the Lord"; (2) it is the "right" thing to do; (3) God commands obedience; and (4) obedience brings a rich reward. Parents are then urged to limit the exercise of their authority and to train their children in the ways of the Lord.

To slaves Paul says, in essence, "Come to view your work as service to Christ, and thus labor for your master in the same way that you would labor for the Lord." To masters Paul says, in essence, "The slave is a person who is to be treated as you expect to be treated, since before God you are both equal."

6:1–3 Paul does not simply command obedience on the part of children. He gives reasons for it. In other words, Paul does not take obedience for granted. In the same way that he addressed husbands and wives (and gave each a rationale for their behavior), he also does the same for children.

6:1 *Children.* The very fact that Paul even addresses children is amazing. Normally, all such instructions would come via their parents. That he addresses children in this public letter means that children were in attendance with their families at worship when such a letter would have been read. Paul does not define a "child" here; i.e., he does not deal with the question of when a child becomes an adult and thus ceases to be under parental authority. This is not a real problem, however, since each culture has its own definition of when adulthood begins. Even as adults, however, children are expected to "honor" their parents.

obey. Paul tells children to "obey" ("follow," "be subject to," literally, "listen to"). He uses a different word from that used when speaking of the relationship between wives and husbands. Parents have authority over their children, but not husbands over wives. Also, although "obey" is a stronger word than "submit," it is not without limits.

in the Lord. This is the first reason children are to obey their parents. There are two ways in which this phrase can be taken: Obey your parents because you are a Christian, and/or obey your parents in everything that is compatible with your commitment to Christ.

for this is right. This is the second of the four reasons Paul gives for obedience. "Children obey parents. That is simply the way it is," Paul says. It is not confined to Christian ethics; it is standard behavior in any society. Pagan moralists, both Greek and Roman, taught it. Stoic philosophers saw a son's obedience as self-prudent, plainly required by reason and part of the "nature of things."

6:2 *"Honor your father and mother."* Paul begins to quote the fifth commandment. This is the third reason children should obey parents. God commands it. "To honor father and mother means more than to obey them, especially if this obedience is interpreted in a merely outward sense. It is the inner attitude of the child toward his parents that comes to the fore in the requirement that he honor them. All selfish obedience or reluctant obedience or obedience under terror is immediately ruled out. To honor implies to love, to regard highly, to show the spirit of respect and consideration. This honor is to be shown to both of the parents, for as far as the child is concerned, they are equal in authority" (Hendriksen).

the first commandment with a promise. Paul probably means "first in importance," since the second commandment (Ex. 20:4–6) promises God's love to those who love God. It has been argued by F. F. Bruce, however, that the second commandment does not contain a promise but a statement of God's character.

6:3 This is the fourth reason for obedience. It produces good rewards. Here, Paul identifies the two aspects of the promise. It involved material well-being and long life. The promise is probably not for individual children, but for the community of which they are a part. It will be prosperous and long-standing.

6:4 Just as children have a duty to obey, parents have the duty to instruct children with gentleness and restraint.

Fathers. The model for a father is that of God, the "Father of all" (Eph. 4:6). In the way that he drew together people from diverse tribes and nations into one loving community (Eph. 3:14–15), so too human fathers are to exercise this kind of love. This view of fatherhood stands in sharp contrast to the harsh Roman father, who had the power of life and death over his children.

exasperate. Parents are to be responsible for not provoking hostility on the part of their children. By humiliating children, being cruel to them, overindulging them, or being unreasonable, parents squash children (rather than encourage them).

bring them up. This verb is literally "nourish" or "feed" them.

training. This word can be translated "discipline," and "is training with the accent on the correction of the young" (Houlden).

instruction. The emphasis here is on what is said verbally to children.

6:5–8 That Paul should even address slaves is amazing. In the first century, they were often considered more akin to farm animals than human beings, the only difference being that they could talk. Slaves were "living tools" according to Aristotle. Yet Paul speaks to them as people able to choose and to decide—quite revolutionary for his era.

SESSION

6

One Flesh

3-PART AGENDA

ICE-BREAKER
15 Minutes

BIBLE STUDY
30 Minutes

CARING TIME
15–45 Minutes

Our marital life is inseparably linked to our sexuality. Certainly marriage is more than sex. Marriage is companionship and shared dreams. Marriage is raising children and sharing life experiences as a family. And marriage is living out a complete personal intimacy that mirrors the intimacy God seeks with all of his children. But at the root of it all was a desire to be one with another person, a drive that is both physical and spiritual. This desire is blessed by God and is good. In Genesis we read, "The man and his wife were both naked, and they felt no shame."

In our fallen state, however, shame has come to be associated with our sexual selves. The church has to take its share of the blame for this. Too often, the church has portrayed sex as something dirty.

God created sex as a wonderful experience that brings both pleasure and intimacy. Sex also makes it possible for us to have children and propagate the species. There is nothing bad or shameful in any of that. Of course, it's true that some people use sex in shameful ways. Instead of being a way to bring intimacy and oneness to marriage, it can be a way of turning people into victims and victimizers. It can be a way of focusing on self and selfish physical need, instead of reaching out and finding union with another person.

LEADER: This is the next to last session in this course. At the end of the course, how would you like to celebrate your time together? With a dinner? With a party? With a commitment to continue as a group?

In this session, we will consider how sex can be maintained as a way to find oneness with our partner, instead of becoming something shameful. In Option 1, we will examine the Bible's love sonnet (the Song of Songs) and use it to affirm the goodness of our sexual lives. In Option 2 (from 1 Corinthians), we will consider what Paul has to say about appropriate sexual expression.

Ice-Breaker / 15 Minutes

Dream Houses. What have you learned about yourself and your marriage while being with this group, and what would be an appropriate house for you and your spouse for your life together? Take turns reading out loud the list below and share the "house" you would choose and why.

SLEEPING BAG FOR TWO: Because you have helped us to get back to the simple things, a simple lifestyle—wide open to the outdoors, the stars, smelling the flowers and listening to the birds again.

GLASS HOUSE: Because you have allowed us to be open and free—to look at the world around, get rid of our rocks, and enjoy life—to let the sun shine in.

SWISS FAMILY ROBINSON TREE HOUSE: Because you have helped us to rebuild our family, work together, see the inner strength in each other, and accept the situation as a new challenge.

GREENWICH VILLAGE APARTMENT: Because you helped us to know each other, to be ourselves, to celebrate the "wild, way-out" side of each other, to care less about conformity and "measuring up" to others' expectations.

LOG CABIN: Because you have affirmed our pioneering spirit that strikes out into unknown expeditions, "homesteading" new frontiers in our spiritual journey.

WINNEBAGO CRUISER: Because you have released in us a desire to travel the "back roads" and to rediscover our heritage—the old watering holes of our childhood and the simple joys of life.

EIGHT-PERSON TENT: Because I want to share more of us with the rest of you. We have become a family together, and there is so much more we can share.

HOUSEBOAT: Because you have started us on a life cruise into uncharted waters and new adventures ... and we would like you to share the adventure with us. The pace will be slower and the facilities a little crowded, but you are all welcome.

PORTABLE SANDBOX: Because you have helped us to discover a child inside that we didn't know was there, and the party is just beginning.

TRAVELING CIRCUS TRAIN: Because you have said it is okay to laugh in the midst of pain, rejoice when times are tough, and celebrate life in all its fullness.

Bible Study / 30 Minutes

Option 1 / Story Passage

Song of Songs 1:16; 2:1–7; 4:1–7 / An Ode to Love

Read Song of Songs 1:16; 2:1–7 and 4:1–7, and discuss the questions which follow with your group. This book was an embarrassment to some theologians during the time when the church had a negative view of sex. They sought to make it simply an allegory for Christ's love for the church. But efforts to remove its literal affirmation of human sexual love fail. Famed theologian Karl Barth called the book an extended commentary on Genesis 2:25: "The man and his wife were both naked, and they felt no shame." (In these passages, "Lover" refers to the words of the man, while "Beloved" refers to the woman's words.)

Beloved

> *[16]How handsome you are, my lover!*
> *Oh, how charming!*
> *And our bed is verdant.*

Beloved

 2
> *I am a rose of Sharon,*
> *a lily of the valleys.*

Lover

> *[2]Like a lily among thorns*
> *is my darling among the maidens.*

Beloved

> *[3]Like an apple tree among the trees of the forest*
> *is my lover among the young men.*
> *I delight to sit in his shade,*
> *and his fruit is sweet to my taste.*
> *[4]He has taken me to the banquet hall,*
> *and his banner over me is love.*
> *[5]Strengthen me with raisins,*
> *refresh me with apples,*
> *for I am faint with love.*
> *[6]His left arm is under my head,*
> *and his right arm embraces me.*

⁷Daughters of Jerusalem, I charge you
by the gazelles and by the does of the field:
Do not arouse or awaken love
until it so desires.

Lover

4 *How beautiful you are, my darling!*
Oh, how beautiful!
Your eyes behind your veil are doves.
Your hair is like a flock of goats
descending from Mount Gilead.
²Your teeth are like a flock of sheep just shorn,
coming up from the washing.
Each has its twin;
not one of them is alone.
³Your lips are like a scarlet ribbon;
your mouth is lovely.
Your temples behind your veil
are like the halves of a pomegranate.
⁴Your neck is like the tower of David,
built with elegance;
on it hang a thousand shields,
all of them shields of warriors.
⁵Your two breasts are like two fawns,
like twin fawns of a gazelle
that browse among the lilies.
⁶Until the day breaks
and the shadows flee,
I will go to the mountain of myrrh
and to the hill of incense.
⁷All beautiful you are, my darling;
there is no flaw in you.

1. When you were in the seventh grade, who did you write a love note about in school? Did you send it to them or keep it to yourself? If you sent it, did you get caught?

2. If you don't know that this reading was from the Bible, which of the following would you think it was?
❏ a love sonnet from the time of Robert and Elizabeth Barrett Browning
❏ some old love notes we wrote in our first year of marriage
❏ love notes from two people who had never been married
❏ the script for a movie from the '40s
❏ words from a tattered page of a book which was passed around in junior high

3. Why do you think God included this in Scripture?
- ❐ It must be some type of symbolic allegory for something more spir-itual.
- ❐ God wanted to affirm the beauty of human sexual love.
- ❐ He wanted a prototype for the Christian romance novel.
- ❐ He didn't want to include it—people slipped this in by mistake.

4. What do you think the woman meant when she said: "Daughters of Jerusalem ... Do not arouse or awaken love until it so desires"?
- ❐ Don't try to "make love happen"—be patient and wait until you know that it's right.
- ❐ Keep yourself pure until married.
- ❐ Love and desire go together.
- ❐ Don't put yourself in a compromising position.
- ❐ other: _____

5. When you were first married, how would you compare your relation-ship to this couple's relationship in Song of Songs?
- ❐ Ours was every bit as romantic.
- ❐ We had some of the same feelings, but didn't know how to put them into words.
- ❐ Our relationship was much more subdued.
- ❐ Our relationship is still this way.
- ❐ other: _____

6. The woman said she was "a rose of Sharon, a lily of the valleys." This was a way of saying that she felt attractive in her husband's pres-ence. The following actions help a person feel more attractive. Which of these does your spouse do the most?
- ❐ tells me how nice I look
- ❐ tells me with their eyes how nice I look
- ❐ brings me romantic gifts
- ❐ brags about me to others
- ❐ displays affection for me
- ❐ leaves me little love notes

7. Which of the actions in the previous question would you like your spouse to do more often?

8. If God's view of sex in marriage is conveyed here, then why do so many couples experience nothing like it?

❏ because they have too much guilt

❏ because they have sexual hang-ups from their past

❏ because they have hang-ups from the church

❏ because sex has been distorted in the media

❏ because they don't work at it

9. Like the couple in this story, what keeps your love alive?

❏ playful teasing

❏ dreaming together

❏ times apart

❏ having caring friends

❏ private rendezvous

10. What positive steps can you take to insure time and privacy to nurture your love life?

❏ Establish a day or a weekend alone every _____.

❏ Go on a "date" every _____.

❏ Plan a romantic trip just for us to _____

❏ other:_____

Option 2 / Epistle Study

1 Cor. 6:12–7:5 / Belonging to Each Other

Paul wrote these instructions to the church at Corinth because the Gentiles there were influenced by Greek religion (which divorced belief in God from any strong moral code in sexual relationships). During that time, in fact, "to Corinthianize" was slang for morally corrupting someone or something. Paul wanted to emphasize that Christians have a higher standard in the marriage relationship.

[12]"Everything is permissible for me"—but not everything is beneficial. "Everything is permissible for me"—but I will not be mastered by anything. [13]"Food for the stomach and the stomach for food"—but God will destroy them both. The body is not meant for sexual immorality, but for the Lord, and the Lord for the body. [14]By his power God raised the Lord from the dead, and he will raise us also. [15]Do you not know that your bodies are members of Christ himself? Shall I then take the members of Christ and unite them with a prostitute? Never! [16]Do you not know that he who unites himself with

a prostitute is one with her in body? For it is said, "The two will become one flesh." ^{17}But he who unites himself with the Lord is one with him in spirit.

^{18}Flee from sexual immorality. All other sins a man commits are outside his body, but he who sins sexually sins against his own body. ^{19}Do you not know that your body is a temple of the Holy Spirit, who is in you, whom you have received from God? You are not your own; ^{20}you were bought at a price. Therefore honor God with your body.

7 *Now for the matter you wrote about: It is good for a man not to marry. ^{2}But since there is so much immorality, each man should have his own wife, and each woman her own husband. ^{3}The husband should fulfill his marital duty to his wife, and likewise the wife to her husband. ^{4}The wife's body does not belong to her alone but also to her husband. In the same way, the husband's body does not belong to him alone but also to his wife. ^{5}Do not deprive each other except by mutual consent and for a time, so that you may devote yourselves to prayer. Then come together again so that Satan will not tempt you because of your lack of self-control.*

1. How do you remember your parents treating the issue of sex when you asked about it?
   ❒ They avoided the subject.
   ❒ They answered every question.
   ❒ They stumbled their way through it.
   ❒ I never asked them.
   ❒ They left it to the school.
   ❒ They left it to the church.
   ❒ They taught me to say "no," but nothing else.
   ❒ other: _____

2. Which of Paul's arguments against sexual immorality are most convincing to you?
   ❒ Sexual sin can enslave ("master") us (v. 12).
   ❒ Sex is more than physical—it's a spiritual union that we should not have with just anyone (vv. 15–16).
   ❒ Sexual sins affect our body (vv. 13,18).
   ❒ Our body is the temple of the Holy Spirit, and what we do with it should honor God (vv. 19–20).

3. How do you react to Paul's teaching that our body is not ours alone, but that our spouse also has a claim on it?
   ❒ Typical male! No one has a claim on my body but me.
   ❒ Fine, but I still have controlling interest.
   ❒ Since he states that the claim is mutual, it's okay.
   ❒ Yes, that's what marriage is about—belonging to each other.

4. Finish this sentence: If couples took seriously Paul's teaching that we should not deprive each other sexually (except by mutual consent and for a short time) ...
   ❐ women would become sex objects again.
   ❐ nobody would ever get any work done.
   ❐ the children would be neglected.
   ❐ sex would become boring and routine.
   ❐ marriages would be on firmer ground.
   ❐ prostitutes would go out of business.
   ❐ people would walk around smiling a lot.
   ❐ couples would feel more fulfilled.

5. How would you rate your ability to discuss sex with your spouse?

1	2	3	4	5	6	7	8	9	10
We never talk about it.			We talk about it when there's a problem.					We talk about it freely.	

6. Why is friendship an important part of a healthy sexual relationship? How are you and your spouse doing at being best friends?

7. What do you think causes adultery?
   ❐ It happens on an impulse.
   ❐ It happens to weak marriages.
   ❐ Our society encourages it.
   ❐ Our sin nature encourages it.
   ❐ other:_____

8. What is your biggest challenge or need regarding your sexuality?
   ❐ expressing what my sexual needs are
   ❐ feeling good about myself
   ❐ putting my sexual past behind me
   ❐ feeling the security of being held
   ❐ being affirmed as an attractive person
   ❐ controlling my impulses
   ❐ other: _____

9. How are you guarding against marital unfaithfulness? How are you ensuring that neither lovemaking nor friendship is neglected in your marriage? What is the next date on the calendar for just the two of you?

Caring Time / 15–45 Minutes

Give everyone a chance to answer the question:

"How can we help you in prayer this week?"

Go around and let each person pray for the person on their right.

P.S. If the next session is your last session together, you may want to plan a party to celebrate your time together. Save a few minutes at the close of this session to make these plans.

Reference Notes

6:12–20 Paul continues to discuss the question of sexuality (see 1 Cor. 5:1–13), here dealing with the issue of prostitution. In so doing, he lays down some general (albeit negative) guidelines.

6:12 *"Everything is permissible for me."* Probably the slogan of a libertarian party at Corinth, which felt that since the body was insignificant (in comparison with the "spirit"), it did not really matter what one did. In one sense, this slogan is true. It defines the nature of Christian freedom, and Paul does not disagree with it. He does take issue with how it has come to be used; i.e., as an excuse for indulgent and promiscuous behavior. He argues that while everything may be permissible, not everything is good (much less beneficial).

mastered. To indulge one's appetites in unsuitable ways is to put oneself under the power of that appetite, and to open the possibility of slavery to a harmful habit. So, in fact, such license is not really Christian liberty because it produces bondage!

6:13 *"Food for the stomach ..."* In this second slogan, the low view of the body also asserts itself. Paul does not directly dispute this slogan, however. Christians are not bound by food laws. Diet is a matter of indifference—especially in that it has no impact on one's salvation.

body. The stomach is one thing (it will pass away in the natural course of things), but the body is something else (it will live on). For Paul, "body" means not just bones and tissues, but the whole person.

not meant for sexual immorality. Paul now qualifies his acceptance of the slogan. It appears, Barrett suggests, that the Corinthians were arguing that in the same way it was permissible for Christians to satisfy their physical appetite without regard to law, so too they had the right to satisfy their sexual appetite with the same disregard of law. This Paul emphatically denies.

6:15 Since the body of the Christian belongs to the Lord, it is inconceivable (*"Never!"*) that it be given over to a prostitute.

prostitute. The reference is probably not just to prostitutes in general (they were numerous in a port city like Corinth), but to temple prostitutes in particular. The Corinthians may have been arguing for the "right" to engage in sexually oriented religious activities.

6:16 ***Do you not know.*** This is no new principle which Paul proposes, as he shows by quoting Genesis 2:24.

one flesh. Such uniting with a prostitute makes the two one flesh. This stands in contrast to the kind of uniting appropriate for holy people, including uniting with the Lord (v. 17).

6:18 ***Flee.*** The temptation to sexual sin was so overwhelming in Corinth that Paul uses this strong verb by way of command.

sexual immorality. Not unexpectedly (given the nature of life in Corinth), the Corinthians were confused about their sexuality. In chapter 7, it appears that many felt marriage should be avoided, and certainly sexual intercourse was to be shunned between marriage partners. So here, the position which Paul is arguing against might be that since it was the duty of a husband to keep his wife "pure," he could occasionally find sexual satisfaction with a harlot if necessary (Barrett).

6:19 In 1 Corinthians 3:16, Paul pointed out that the church was the dwelling place of the Holy Spirit. Here he points to the parallel truth: so, too, is the individual believer.

6:20 ***bought at a price.*** The image is of ransoming slaves from their bondage. In the same way, Christ has paid the ransom price in order to free Christians from the bondage of sin. Out of sheer gratitude, Christians ought to flee sin. Out of sheer common sense, they should flee sin, lest they fall back into bondage.

7:1–5 Paul now addresses another problem in his letter. It concerns married (or once-married) people.

7:1 ***you wrote about.*** Up to this point Paul has been dealing with matters reported to him, but now he responds to a series of concerns about which the Corinthian Christians have written asking his advice.

to marry. The phrase is literally "to touch a woman," and is a common euphemism for sexual intercourse. "Nowhere in the ancient world is this phrase used to mean 'get married' " (Fee).

It is good for a man not to marry. This statement probably ought to be put in quotation marks (as in 6:12–13): "It is good for a man not to touch a woman." It is quite possibly a slogan that reflects the position of an ascetic group within the Corinthian church which felt that Christian husbands who wanted to be really spiritual ought to refrain from sexual intercourse with their wives. Or, Paul may have been responding to a question from the Corinthians along the lines of "Is it bad for a man not to marry?"

7:2: First, Paul says that it is not good for a husband and a wife to abstain from sexual relationship, since this will just increase the temptation to commit adultery.

have his own wife. The phrase mans "to be married," or "to have sexual relations" (Fee).

7:3–4 Paul now gives the reasons for his views: There is to be complete mutuality within marriage in the matter of sexual rights. This statement stands in sharp contrast to the consensus of the first century, which understood that it was the husband alone who had sexual rights and the wife simply submitted to him.

7:5 This is the negative form of the commandment in verses 3–4. Abstinence is allowed under two conditions: both partners agree, and it is for a limited time.

prayer. The purpose of such abstinence is prayer.

lack of self-control. Paul assumes that a couple would not be married in the first place if they did not feel any sexual desire, and thus they ought to fulfill such desires legitimately, lest they be tempted to adultery.

3-PART AGENDA

ICE-BREAKER
15 Minutes

BIBLE STUDY
30 Minutes

CARING TIME
15–45 Minutes

Till Death Do Us Part

Commitment has become a rather difficult issue today, especially among "baby boomers." Divorce has hit epidemic proportions—it seems like every life has been touched in some way by divorce. If something doesn't change, the couple who actually lives up to the vow "till death do us part" will become the exception rather than the rule.

Part of the problem seems to be that we live in a "What's in it for me?" culture. Once marriage becomes a situation where the "profit–loss" balance sheet no longer seems to be "in the black," some feel it is time to bail out as if they were selling a falling stock.

LEADER: Read the bottom part of page M8 in the center section concerning future mission possibilities for your group. Save plenty of time for the evaluation and future planning during the Caring Time. You will need to be prepared to lead this important discussion.

Whether divorce should ever really be an option for Christians could probably be debated for a long time. But it is clear that God's intent is for marriage to be "till death do us part." Such commitment to each other is scriptural. And it also gives people a sense of security, knowing that marriage is a relationship on which they can rely.

In this session, we will talk about the commitment we have made to each other—the commitment of marriage. In Option 1, we will discuss an incident when Jesus said some strong things about the importance of commitment in marriage. In Option 2, we will look at part of the well-known "Love Chapter"—1 Corinthians 13.

Ice-Breaker / 15 Minutes

Second Honeymoon. Let each person answer the following questions.

1. If you had $1,000 to splurge for a second honeymoon, how would you spend it?
❏ one glorious weekend in a luxury hotel
❏ one week in a nice hotel
❏ two weeks sightseeing and staying in economy hotels
❏ three weeks in the boondocks sleeping in the back of the car
❏ save the money

2. If you could take along something or someone to pass the time (along with your spouse), what or who would you take?
❏ my laptop computer   ❏ some good books
❏ my mother   ❏ my video-collection
❏ my golf clubs   ❏ an old buddy
❏ my cell phone   ❏ nothing—I'll be too busy.

Bible Study / 30 Minutes

Option 1 / Gospel Study

Matthew 19:1–12 / A Trick Question

19 When Jesus had finished saying these things, he left Galilee and went into the region of Judea to the other side of the Jordan. *²Large crowds followed him, and he healed them there.*

³Some Pharisees came to him to test him. They asked, "Is it lawful for a man to divorce his wife for any and every reason?"

⁴"Haven't you read," he replied, "that at the beginning the Creator 'made them male and female,' ⁵and said, 'For this reason a man will leave his father and mother and be united with his wife, and the two will become one flesh'? ⁶So they are no longer two, but one. Therefore what God has joined together, let man not separate."

⁷"Why then," they asked, "did Moses command that a man give his wife a certificate of divorce and send her away?"

⁸Jesus replied, "Moses permitted you to divorce your wives because your hearts were hard. But it was not this way from the beginning. ⁹I tell you that anyone who divorces his wife, except for marital unfaithfulness, and marries another woman commits adultery."

[10]The disciples said to him, "If this is the situation between a husband and wife, it is better not to marry."

[11]Jesus replied, "Not everyone can accept this word, but only those to whom it has been given. [12]For some are eunuchs because they were born that way; others were made that way by men; and others have renounced marriage because of the kingdom of heaven. The one who can accept this should accept it."

1. What premarital advice do you remember from your parents? Has any of it proven to be true?

2. Why did the Pharisees test Jesus?
   ❐ They wanted him to teach heresy.
   ❐ They wanted to undermine his credibility.
   ❐ They wanted to turn the people against him.
   ❐ They wanted to show that they knew more than Jesus.

3. Why do you think they chose a question on divorce?
   ❐ because divorce was a controversial issue
   ❐ because they were trying to divide the men and women
   ❐ because they were genuinely looking for an answer
   ❐ because they knew it was a "trick question"

4. How would you summarize Jesus' attitude toward marriage?
   ❐ Marriage is ordained by God.
   ❐ Marriage is a lifelong commitment.
   ❐ Marriage means to "leave and cleave."
   ❐ If marriage doesn't work, "bail out."
   ❐ Marriage is holy, but has been made unholy by some who join this institution.

5. How would you summarize Jesus' attitude toward divorce?
   ❐ Divorce is a result of selfishness.
   ❐ Divorce is a perversion of God's ideal for marriage.
   ❐ Divorce is permissible when unfaithfulness is involved.
   ❐ Divorce is settling for "second best."
   ❐ Divorce can be the "lesser of two evils."

6. What would Jesus say is necessary for a couple to have a fulfilling, solid marriage?

"Some of the most deeply happy married couples I have known have found their happiness in pursuing together the destiny which they deeply believed they had come to share. For people of deep religious faith this need in marriage is ideally met. Such couples see their love as partaking of, and reflecting back, the love of God."
—David R. Mace

7. Answer true (T) or false (F) to the following statements and discuss your responses with your group.

___ A strong marriage relationship, once broken, is very difficult to restore.

___ A marriage must change over time if it is to survive.

___ Marriage can supply all of our relationship needs.

___ A marriage can be good without being intimate.

___ Men more than women lose their identity in a marriage relationship.

8. What would help you to have the marriage that God desires?

Option 2 / Epistle Study

1 Corinthians 13:1–7 / Maturing Love

13 *And now I will show you the most excellent way. If I speak in the tongues of men and of angels, but have not love, I am only a resounding gong or a clanging cymbal. ²If I have the gift of prophecy and can fathom all mysteries and all knowledge, and if I have a faith that can move mountains, but have not love, I am nothing. ³If I give all I possess to the poor and surrender my body to the flames, but have not love, I gain nothing.*

⁴Love is patient, love is kind. It does not envy, it does not boast, it is not proud. ⁵It is not rude, it is not self-seeking, it is not easily angered, it keeps no record of wrongs. ⁶Love does not delight in evil but rejoices with the truth. ⁷It always protects, always trusts, always hopes, always perseveres.

1. How easy is it for you to tell or show someone you love them?

2. What type of love is Paul writing about in these verses?

3. Why is love more important than eloquent speech, superior knowledge, and sacrificial giving?

4. In verses 4 through 7, what are the major characteristics and responsibilities of love?

5. In your group, give yourself a checkup on the description of perfect love in verses 4–7. Let one person read out loud the first phrase below and then have everyone call out a number from 1 to 10 to indicate how you would rank your own life on that characteristic. Then read out loud the next phrase and have everyone call out another number, etc. through the list.

LOVE IS PATIENT: I don't take out my frustrations on those I love. I am calm under pressure and careful with my tongue.

| 1 | 2 | 3 | 4 | 5 | 6 | 7 | 8 | 9 | 10 |

LOVE IS KIND: I go out of my way to say nice words and do thoughtful things for others.

| 1 | 2 | 3 | 4 | 5 | 6 | 7 | 8 | 9 | 10 |

LOVE DOES NOT ENVY: I am not envious of others' gifts and abilities or of what they have. Neither am I jealous with my time toward those who need me.

| 1 | 2 | 3 | 4 | 5 | 6 | 7 | 8 | 9 | 10 |

LOVE DOES NOT BOAST: I don't consider my role any more important than those I love—or talk like "I know better."

| 1 | 2 | 3 | 4 | 5 | 6 | 7 | 8 | 9 | 10 |

LOVE IS NOT RUDE: I don't make cutting or crude remarks when I don't get my way—or become silent and withdrawn.

| 1 | 2 | 3 | 4 | 5 | 6 | 7 | 8 | 9 | 10 |

LOVE IS NOT SELF-SEEKING: I don't put myself first. I try to give those I love spiritual and emotional support.

| 1 | 2 | 3 | 4 | 5 | 6 | 7 | 8 | 9 | 10 |

LOVE IS NOT EASILY ANGERED: I don't let little things bother me, especially with those I love. I have a muffler on my mouth.

| 1 | 2 | 3 | 4 | 5 | 6 | 7 | 8 | 9 | 10 |

LOVE KEEPS NO RECORD OF WRONGS: I don't keep score of the number of times those I love have said something or done something that upset me, and I don't bring it up when we have a conflict or disagreement.

| 1 | 2 | 3 | 4 | 5 | 6 | 7 | 8 | 9 | 10 |

Caring Time / 15–45 Minutes

1. Take some time to evaluate the life of your group by using the state-ments below. Read the first sentence out loud and ask everyone to explain where they would put a dot between the two extremes. When you are finished, go back and give your group an overall grade in the categories of Group Building, Bible Study and Mission.

GROUP BUILDING

On celebrating life and having fun together, we were more like a ...
wet blanket _____**hot tub**

On becoming a caring community, we were more like a ...
prickly porcupine _____**cuddly teddy bear**

BIBLE STUDY

On sharing our spiritual stories, we were more like a ...
shallow pond _____**spring-fed lake**

On digging into Scripture, we were more like a ...
slow-moving snail _____**voracious anteater**

MISSION

On inviting new people into our group, we were more like a ...
barbed-wire fence _____**wide-open door**

On stretching our vision for mission, we were more like an ...
ostrich _____**eagle**

2. What are some specific areas in which you have grown in this course about strengthening your marriage?
❏ handling pressures and making our marriage a top priority
❏ understanding each other and constructively handling our differ-ences
❏ appreciating our past and learning from the hard times
❏ relating to our children and extended families
❏ making sex and romance an integral part of our marriage
❏ affirming regularly our lasting commitment to each other
❏ other:_____

A covenant is a promise made to each other in the presence of God. Its purpose is to indicate your intention to make yourselves available to one another for the fulfillment of the purposes you share in common. In a spirit of prayer, work your way through the following sentences, trying to reach an agreement on each statement pertaining to your ongoing life together. Write out your covenant like a contract, stating your purpose, goals and the ground rules for your group.

1. The purpose of our group will be ... (finish the sentence)

2. Our goals will be ...

3. We will meet for _____weeks, after which we will decide if we wish to continue as a group.

4. We will meet from _____ to _____ and we will strive to start on time and end on time.

5. We will meet at _____ (place) or we will rotate from house to house.

6. We will agree to the following ground rules for our group (check):

   ❐ PRIORITY: While you are in the course, you give the group meetings priority.

   ❐ PARTICIPATION: Everyone participates and no one dominates.

   ❐ RESPECT: Everyone is given the right to their own opinion, and all questions are encouraged and respected.

   ❐ CONFIDENTIALITY: Anything that is said in the meeting is never repeated outside the meeting.

   ❐ EMPTY CHAIR: The group stays open to new people at every meeting, as long as they understand the ground rules.

   ❐ SUPPORT: Permission is given to call upon each other in time of need at any time.

   ❐ ACCOUNTABILITY: We agree to let the members of the group hold us accountable to the commitments which each of us make in whatever loving ways we decide upon.

   ❐ MISSION: We will do everything in our power to start a new group.

13:1–3 If a person does not love, neither spiritual gifts, nor good deeds, nor martyrdom is of any ultimate value to that person. Love is the context within which these gifts and deeds become significant.

13:1 *tongues of men and of angels.* Ecstatic speech—highly prized in Corinth—is an authentic gift of the Holy Spirit; however, it becomes like the unintelligible noise of pagan worship when used outside the context of love.

gong / cymbal. Paul is probably thinking of the repetitious and meaningless noise generated at pagan temples by beating on metal instruments.

13:2 Paul contrasts three other spiritual gifts with love: prophecy, knowledge and faith.

prophecy. Such activity is highly commended by Paul (e.g., 1 Cor. 14:1); yet without love even a prophet is really nothing.

fathom all mysteries. In Corinth, special, esoteric knowledge was highly prized (1 Cor. 1:18–2:16), but even if one knew the very secrets of God, without love it would be to no end. That which makes a person significant (i.e., the opposite of nothing) is not a gift like prophecy or knowledge, but it is the ability to love.

faith that can move mountains. Paul refers to Jesus' words in Mark 11:23—even such massive faith that can unleash God's power in visible ways is not enough to make a person significant without love at its foundation.

13:3 *give all I possess to the poor.* Presumably Paul refers to goods and property given to others, but not in love. The point is not: do not give if you cannot do so in love (the poor still profit from the gifts regardless of the spirit in which they are given), but rather that the loveless giver gains no reward on the Day of Judgment.

surrender my body. Not even the act of the martyr—giving up one's very life for the sake of another or in a great cause—brings personal benefit when it is done outside love.

13:4–7 By way of definition, Paul tells us what love does and does not do. He defines love in terms of action and attitude.

13:4 *patient.* This word describes patience with people (not circumstances). It characterizes the person who is slow to anger (long-suffering) despite provocation.

kind. In fact, the loving person does good to those who provoke them.

not envy. The loving person does not covet what others have nor begrudge them their possessions.

not boast. The loving person is self-effacing, not a braggart.

not proud. Literally, not "puffed up." The loving person does not feel others to be inferior, nor do they look down on people.

13:5 *not rude.* The same (Greek) word is used in 1 Corinthians 7:36 to describe a man who led on a woman but then refused to marry her.

not self-seeking. The loving person not only does not insist on their rights, but will give up their due for the sake of others.

not easily angered. The loving person is not easily angered by others; they are not touchy.

keeps no record of wrongs. The verb is an accounting term and the image is of a ledger sheet on which wrongs received are recorded. The loving person forgives and forgets.

13:6 *does not delight in evil.* The loving person does not rejoice when others fail (which could make them feel superior) or enjoy pointing out wrong in others.

rejoices with the truth. Paul shifts back to the positive.

13:7 *protects.* Literally, "to put a cover over." The loving person is concerned with how to shelter other people from harm.

trusts. Literally, "believes all things"; i.e., "never loses faith."

hopes. Loves does not lose hope.

perseveres. Love keeps loving despite hardship.